Advance Praise for *Riding on Faith*

"This is a compelling read! Anyone interested in ministry and missions whose body temperature is more or less ninety-eight degrees will be into the story by page 3. The compelling secret in this story is that God doesn't recruit superheroes of the faith. He recruits common, ordinary men and women who are willing to let Him do His work through them, and He makes them heroes of the faith."

STEVE SAINT
Founder and president of Indigenous Peoples Technology & Education Center (ITEC)

"What a story! Alice Teisan is a living example of how to turn adversity into opportunity, suffering into service, and disappointment into dreams-come-true."

KEVIN MILLER
Former executive vice president of Christianity Today

"When I interviewed Alice for the radio program *First Person*, we met in the workshop of His Wheels International, where volunteers were building trikes and repairing bikes. As Alice told me her story of overcoming physical challenges, the phrase that kept running through my mind were the apostle Paul's words: 'I can do all things through him who strengthens me.' You'll enjoy reading this remarkable story of overcoming adversity through faith in Christ and a God-given vision to serve others."

WAYNE SHEPHERD
Christian radio host

"Alice Teisan's chronicling the history of His Wheels is a wonderful mix of taking on the nuts and bolts of building hand trikes accompanied by the spiritual blessings of her call. Like so many adventures of faith, His Wheels has allowed Alice to venture into uncharted waters of trust."

BOB DAVENPORT
Founder and director of Wandering Wheels

"[Alice is] an unbelievably exceptional nurse who you will find has many not-so-hidden talents portrayed within the covers of this book. You will be delighted and thrilled as you encounter the mighty working of the God of the universe."

HAROLD PAUL ADOLPH, MD FACS
President of St. Luke's Health Care Foundation

"Looking way beyond her tough circumstances, just like she had to on our cross-country bike trek, Alice followed the path through the wilderness that the Lord made and came out to the beautiful valley on the other side, where she has discovered how to joyfully use her love of biking to give mobility and dignity to others through her ministry."

CARLA KOONTZ
Executive director of the Center for Global Studies and Initiatives, Spring Arbor University

"Alice rides by faith every day, and so can we. Hounded by confusion, anger, helplessness, and loss of control, she shows us how to navigate the rocky road of adversity by trusting God, for whom pain is never malicious or wasted. As founder and CEO of HIS Wheels, an organization dedicated to manufacturing and delivering specialized bikes, Alice is able to help those who once were doomed to immobility but who now soar on wheels that must seem like wings of eagles!"

C. CHARLES W. LEWIS, PHD
Clinical psychologist and founder of Barnabas International

"There are few stories that are as wonderfully inspiring as Alice's. This is God's story of faithfulness to a woman whose passion and vision have made the world a better place. Alice stood the test and was found faithful. I highly recommend this book. You will not be disappointed."

DAVID SVEEN
Founder and president of Cedarstone Partners; adjunct professor at Wheaton College

Riding on Faith

Keeping Your Balance When the Wheels Fall Off

Alice Teisan

Riding on Faith: Keeping Your Balance When the Wheels Fall Off

Published by Alice Teisan, Wheaton, Illinois 60187.

Back cover photo of Ethiopian man on trike thanks to Soddo Christian Hospital.

Cover designed by Frank Bargerhuff

Edited by Stephanie Rische

Library of Congress Cataloging-in-PublicationData: 2012917324

ISBN-13: 978-0988273504   ISBN-10: 0988273500

To my nephew, Benjamin

Great is the LORD, and greatly to be praised; and his greatness is unsearchable. One generation shall praise thy works to another, and shall declare thy mighty acts. I will speak of the glorious honour of thy majesty, and of thy wondrous works.

(Psalm 145:3-5, KJV)

Contents

Pedaling with a Passion

For my sweet sixteenth birthday my twin brother and only sibling, Dan, gave me a small jewelry box. When I saw it my heart fluttered with an excitement I'd never experienced before. Anticipation welled up inside me as I touched the plush velvet and began opening it. The sparkle in my eyes bounced off the brushed gold wheels of a beautiful, detailed bicycle pendant hanging from a delicate gold chain necklace.

When I saw it I wondered, *How did my brother get the idea to buy me such a perfect tailor-made gift? Will I ever find the words to properly convey how special he has just made me feel?*

While trying to express my feelings of gratitude, I fumbled to get the necklace out of the box. I needed help! So Dan took it out of the box, undid the clasp, and hung my first piece of jewelry around my neck. I knew then that I would feel this special every time I wore it. Through this gift, Dan was making sure my passion for exploring the world, perched upon a bicycle seat, became part of my everyday fashion.

While I was trying to contain the joy and elation bubbling up from within, Dan still had another surprise waiting. The necklace was accompanied by a promise, guaranteeing my life's purpose would one day include cycling. "When I get rich, I'll buy you a bicycle shop!"

Inside I wondered, *What did he just say? Did I hear him right? Who told Dan the secret hidden in my heart before I had even identified it myself?*

The once-hidden secret that Dan uncovered was one I could never ignore again. I would spend the next several decades on a desperate search, trying to find that dream. I had no idea how long and winding that road would be, and what kind of potholes lay ahead. But God did.

Countdown

The countdown had begun. It was July 23, 1992. In four days I would be heading out on a ten-day, one-thousand-mile bicycle trip from Illinois to Delaware. I couldn't wait. For me, bicycling was synonymous with open roads, adventures, and creating lasting memories.

I had just turned thirty, and by that point cycling was firmly woven into the matrix of my life. I had already bicycled ten thousand miles, on four continents. I had ridden from coast to coast across the United States twice and around England and Scotland while still in high school. Later I'd ridden in Zimbabwe, Israel, Florida, and the Canadian Rockies. I looked forward with great anticipation to the upcoming adventure awaiting me. As I prepared for the trip, my mind wandered back to some of my early bicycling memories.

It's no exaggeration to say that my first experiences on a bicycle helped establish the foundation of my life. At the age of five, I learned to ride a two-wheeler in just one day. This incident revealed my personality as a goal setter with the fierce determination to accomplish whatever I set my mind to. While riding the next day, my bicycle broke in half. I cried all the way home, lugging the broken parts of the bicycle my dad had gleaned from the trash less than twenty-four hours earlier.

Later that same afternoon my dad said, "Okay, let's go buy you a new bike." I still remember how the jittery feeling of excitement washed away my sadness as we hopped in the car and headed off to Jake's Bike Store. My eyes scanned the shop and landed on a brilliant purple Schwinn "Lil Chik" bicycle with a glittery silver-colored banana seat that was soon to be mine. Going to Jake's was the first link in my bicycle dream chain of events.

After breaking in my "Lil Chik" with a few trips around the block, I grew bored. The next time around, my competitive athletic spirit shone through as I tested my bicycle limits. With an ever-increasing rotation of the pedals, I started turning the handlebars from side to side until I lost control. My chin hit the pavement, marking the spot with my blood. The crash dictated the next new adventure—to the hospital emergency room for stitches. But that didn't squelch my fast-growing passion. Instead, my adventures just kept getting bigger.

Only weeks later I was off to the local candy store, about a mile away. When I came out of the store, my bicycle was gone. I walked home crying, looking around and hoping someone had simply stashed it in the bushes. As I continued walking, something much stronger than sadness surfaced. I started looking at people with suspicion, wondering if they had stolen my bike. Later I would learn that this theft was an object lesson, warning me that a significant loss has the power to alter my view of the world, if I let it. I found myself grappling with the concept of forgiveness, even though I couldn't fully articulate it back then.

When the alarm went off that warm July morning, I jumped out of bed. I had already submitted the necessary paperwork to ensure the best care for the patients I treated in my role as a home health nurse. Now it was time for the fun part—informing them of my upcoming vacation.

But while tending to my morning routines, I was struck by a violent, three-hour, flu-like diarrhea episode. Completely drained, I tried walking to the phone, but the room was spinning so fast I fell to the ground. Too weak to move and racked with stomach cramps and body aches, I curled up in a ball and closed my eyes to rest. It didn't work. All alone in my apartment, I slithered to the phone on my stomach without the strength to even crawl. Out of obligation, I phoned my boss. "I'm too sick to work today," I whispered faintly. "I can't even tell you the routine patients who need a substitute."

I was crushed. How could an illness strike me this close to my trip? I was in excellent physical condition, having spent many summer nights playing tennis. In preparation for the trip I had also been running eighteen miles a week and biking forty to sixty miles a week.

Trying to think positively in spite of my horrific day, I was glad this bug was hitting now instead of four or five days later when I was on the road. Now there was still time for the flu to run its course, leaving a couple of days to regain my energy. I spent the day in bed, overcome by an agonizing, bone-deep, generalized pain. It was the worst pain and weakness I'd ever experienced, making it tough to navigate the short treks from my bedroom to the bathroom and then on to the kitchen for fluids. But I forced myself, knowing I needed to push fluids if my body was going to regain the necessary strength to get back on track.

Throughout the day, in an attempt to distract myself from the excruciating pain, I wandered down several bicycle memory lanes. Seven months earlier, in January, I had gone on a weeklong trip in Florida with Wandering Wheels, a Christian bicycling group I had done most of my cycling tours with. While there, I had tried out a used custom Schwinn Paramount that a Wandering Wheels leader was selling. It fit perfectly. Even though I tried to convince myself that I was content with my old bike, I didn't succeed.

Three months later I drove to the Wandering Wheels headquarters in Upland, Indiana, to buy the $1,200 fluorescent yellow bike, equipped with a triple-front mountain crank and a large-ranged seven-speed cog, providing the necessary gear ratio for handling coast-to-coast terrain. I was looking forward to finally riding a bike that fit, complete with state-of-the-art equipment and my first set of clipless pedals.

Buying the bike was extravagant for me, but then again, this bike trip was the first step on a planned career change. If all went according to plan, I would soon be headed off to work with Wandering Wheels. I was getting ready to leave behind my successful, full-time, home health nursing position at Rush Presbyterian St. Luke's Medical Center, one of Chicago's most prestigious hospitals. I would also leave behind the part-time position as a cardiac rehabilitation nurse that I'd held since 1988 at West Suburban Hospital Medical Center.

The one-thousand-mile trip was the final leg of a coast-to-coast trip already in progress. For Wandering Wheels and me, it was a ten-day interview. In my mind I already had the next month planned out. When I returned home, I would submit my resignation to Rush, pack up my belongings, and move to the small town of Upland. I hadn't considered the logistics like where I'd live once I got there. The thought of heading off to work with Wandering Wheels squeezed out all fears and doubts. It didn't bother me to leave behind a salary that only ten months earlier had made me think, *Wow, I could live the rest of my life comfortably off this!*

Pursuing full-time Christian ministry was something I had wanted to do since finishing high school. I thought working with Wandering Wheels would provide me the opportunity to combine my cycling passion and my dream of full-time Christian ministry.

As I lay in bed that day I desperately wanted to believe all I had was the twenty-four-hour flu. But deep down, I suspected worse.

Detour

The "twenty-four-hour flu" left me tossing and turning to find a comfortable position. A sharp pain in my right shoulder blade made turning my head nearly impossible. A continuous ache at the lowest part of my back meant it was intolerable to remain in one position. The bone-deep pain throughout my body was getting worse with each passing day. Restful, restorative sleep had been chased away, replaced by chronic insomnia. I felt like a terrorist had invaded my body and was destroying every organ and system in it.

I suffered general disorientation, impaired concentration, and difficulty processing words, compounded by a hangover-type brain fog that made it hard to recall common words while trying to form cohesive sentences. I worried, *Was I facing early onset dementia?*

I also experienced auditory and visual hypersensitivity. The ticking kitchen clock bothered me so much that I had to remove the battery. The sirens outside my rented attic apartment in Chicago now seemed excruciatingly amplified. Due to these new challenges, I was unable to talk on the phone, listen to the radio, or even engage in conversation. In addition, I couldn't tolerate natural sunlight, indoor lighting, or the images on television. My severe limitations created loneliness and isolation, and it wasn't long before I found myself in an emotionally fragile state.

At the onset of the "flu," I felt dizzy but assumed it was due to dehydration; my background in nursing led me to believe it would self-correct with fluids. Not so! Instead, I also began to experience faintness and lightheadedness that worsened when I changed positions—from lying down to a sitting up, from sitting to standing. My erratic and fast heartbeat left me feeling weak, as if I were biking coast-to-coast nonstop. When walking, I felt woozy and ricocheted like a pinball from one wall to another.

I felt like someone had plugged me into a slow cooker with a broken thermostat. I hoped my continuous low-grade fever, severe night sweats, and overactive intestinal and urinary systems were burning up and ejecting the foreign invader that was causing my sickness. It didn't happen. Instead, I was left with a ravenous appetite, as if my blood sugar were constantly low. Fear overcame me. I wondered, *Is my body rejecting my organs or shutting down?* As a nurse, I knew such a condition existed, but no one had ever described to me how it felt.

In the past, I'd often wondered what would happen if I became ill and unable to care for myself while single and living alone. Now my greatest fear had come true. I didn't have any close friends or family nearby. I'd lived in my apartment for four years, but I wasn't home much. My friends were scattered over a twenty-mile radius, and I attended a mega-church fifteen miles away. Two of my cousins lived near the church, but my immediate family all lived in the Detroit area, three hundred miles away.

Terrified, I pondered, *What's wrong with me? Am I dying? Do I have cancer? Let me out of this body!* By the end of the third day, I contemplated going to the emergency room. However, after eight years of experience as a nurse, I knew the reception I'd receive. There was no way to evaluate, test, or medically verify such invisible, vague subjective symptoms.

As I role-played a nurse/patient discussion in my head, I knew a trip to the ER would be disastrous. If *I* were the nurse, I could picture myself saying, "Okay ma'am, calm down. Let's discuss one problem at a time." But as the patient, I would only be able to blurt out one random, unrelated symptom after another. As a nurse, I'd leave the room exasperated and in search of sanity, wondering if I was as messed up as my patient. Fearing the collegiate critique of my assessment skills, I would engage in a "professional conferencing" conversation. "Beware! Room 2 is the craziest whacked-out thirty-year-old hypochondriac I've ever encountered. She needs to get a life! She's crying to us when we're trying to deal with real, life-threatening emergencies." As a patient, I needed to find help somewhere.

After ruling out a trip to the ER, I turned to a lesson I'd learned perched upon a bicycle seat.

It was January 1988, when I was twenty-six. The place was Israel. The trip had begun on New Year's Day, when a friend took my bike and me to Chicago's O'Hare International Airport. My bike was boxed and protected with my sleeping bag and pillow. All forty team members dropped our bikes at a special cargo area before proceeding to the check-in counter. The rest of my gear for the twenty-four-day trip was crammed into my carry-on bicycle pannier luggage. Once in Israel, we carried the bicycle panniers on our bikes while the rented follow-up minivan carried our sleeping gear.

We arrived midday on Shabbat, Israel's holy day, which begins on Friday at sundown and ends at sundown on Saturday. I was hungry and ready to explore Jerusalem in search of food, but by the time the shops reopened, jet lag had set in. According to my body's clock, it was the wee hours of the morning. I wanted bed instead of breakfast.

The next day we began a four-day walking tour through Jerusalem, led by a local college-educated tour guide. What I saw at the sites wasn't what I'd imagined after years of listening to sermons, reading Scripture, and singing hymns. The biblical sites were commercialized, full of incense burners and gaudy decorations. These may have been meant as forms of religious honor, but to me they cheapened the sacredness of the sites. It wasn't until a team leader challenged us to identify the holy thing behind the holy place that I was able to refocus my thoughts.

We stopped at the Western Wall, which was known as the Wailing Wall before the Six Day War in 1967. "For centuries, especially on the 9th of Av, the anniversary of the Temple's destruction, the Jews would flock to the wall to moan their treasured loss."[1] I was moved while observing the dedication of the Jews who went there daily to pray.

At the Garden of Gethsemane, I was reminded of Jesus' words to Peter in that same place. "'Sit here while I pray. . . . My soul is very sorrowful, even to death. Remain here and watch.' And going a little farther, [Jesus] fell on the ground and prayed. . . . And he came and found them sleeping, and he said to Peter, 'Simon, are you asleep? Could you not watch one hour?'"[2]

After only four days in Israel, I was haunted by the concept of prayer. I had gone to Israel grappling with my faith. I grew up in a Christian home and had accepted Christ at the age of twelve. But now, at the age of twenty-six, I was at a critical juncture. I knew I had to either commit myself completely to Christ or walk away from faith altogether.

On the fifth day our Wandering Wheels leader began with group devotions, reading Psalm 121:1-2: "I lift up my eyes to the hills. From where does my help come? My help comes from the LORD, who made heaven and earth."[3] We were ready to begin cycling out of Jerusalem and were looking up toward the Judean Hills. He encouraged us to look up to heaven, like David did, when the road got tough.

Only minutes after beginning to ride, I met with an ever-increasing resistance on my pedals as we headed upward. I was hot, sweaty, and exhausted, having already shifted into my easiest gear. Knowing I still had fifty miles of uphill terrain ahead of me provided countless opportunities to practice looking up to God. Little did I know then, in a few short years I would desperately need to rely on this lesson again.

Months later, after returning from Israel, I heard a sermon by Pastor Lutzer of Moody Church in Chicago. He posed the same question to the congregation that Jesus had asked His disciples: "Can you not pray with Me one hour?" It reminded me of thoughts I'd jotted in my journal while on my Israel trip: "I'd hate to have Jesus return and hear Him say, 'Alice could you not pray with me for one hour?'" I knew the pastor's sermon was just for me, so I left church and went home to begin my prayer journey. I had decided to pray one uninterrupted hour a day. My grocery list of prayers only took two minutes. With fifty-eight minutes remaining, which felt like an eternity, all the distractions of life rushed in and I couldn't concentrate. I realized I didn't have any idea how to pray.

Over the years I had found it much easier to pray while perched on a bicycle seat traveling through God's schoolroom of nature. The different parts of the holy symphonic performance engaged all my senses there. Rushing waves, buzzing bugs, rustling leaves, and gusting headwinds all sang God's praises. The swaying trees, flying birds, and people sauntering along the road were an invitation for my heart to dance before the Lord. The blue skies that dazzled with cloud formations and the vibrant colors of a rainbow reminded me of God's faithfulness to His people. The sweet fragrances that oozed from the flowers, the freshness of the forest pines, and the salty air of the ocean shores made me long for my prayers to be counted as incense before the Lord. While traversing the hills and vales, the twinges throughout my muscle fibers, the rhythmic beat of my heart, and the exhalation of air from my lungs reminded me to give thanks for the body God had so fearfully and wonderfully made. Feeling the sun's penetrating rays while sweat dripped from my brow made basking in the Sun of Righteousness almost palpable. I knew I could never exhaust the vast expanse of prayer while riding.

But that afternoon at my bedside was a different story. After my first attempt, I modified my goal to one uninterrupted hour a week, providing time to build my prayer muscles while adding to the lessons I'd learned in God's outdoor sanctuary.

Now on the third miserable bedridden day of my illness I cried, "Lord, have mercy. Don't abandon me. I need You now like never before." I wondered how I would make it through another day. It was then I decided to pray one uninterrupted hour a day, making it my number-one occupation. Even though the wheels fell off my rolling bicycle "prayer altar" and came to a standstill at my bedside, the God I prayed to would never change. I was starting to realize that prayer was the only way I'd make it through another day.

It was my fourth symptom-filled day—the day before I was supposed to join the rest of the team for the Wandering Wheels trip. But instead I was embarking on a different adventure. The first trip out of my house was to see my internist, Dr. Vesna Skul, the Director of Women's Medicine at Rush. I couldn't have foreseen the trouble I'd experience driving to Dr. Skul's office, only six miles away.

Just a few blocks from home, brain fogginess set in, and it was compounded by a severe, concussion-like headache. This resulted in tunnel vision and delayed reaction time, making driving difficult and dangerous.

Ten months earlier, when I began working at Rush, I did my homework before choosing a primary physician. I talked with several colleagues, and Dr. Skul was their top recommendation. During my initial visit she spent an hour taking a comprehensive history and performing a thorough examination, complete with baseline laboratory work. I was impressed by her professional manner, communication skills, knowledge base, and respect for me as a colleague.

This time, however, I ended up waiting over an hour in the exam room before seeing Dr. Skul. During that time I began to feel worse than I had felt at home. My face turned fire-engine red. I felt nauseous and my anxiety rose. As the wait time mounted, so did my anger. But it wasn't just the delay. For the first time I was experiencing the intense emotions related to my loss of health.

What I didn't know then was that the physical symptoms I experienced at the doctor's office were the result of a heat intolerance. Within minutes of being in a warm building or out in the sun, I would become dizzy. My cognitive skills would elude me. My heart rate would rise, leaving me feeling faint. My body would begin to tremble, and my hands would shake uncontrollably as if I had advanced Parkinson's disease.

In addition to all that, I was now experiencing hypersensitivity to the air quality and airflow, along with the chemicals, allergens, and molds in the building. So by the time Dr. Skul entered the room, I was a mess. And at the time I didn't know why.

She greeted me with a warm embrace and showed compassion and care while listening to my symptoms. She understood that I was a nurse by profession, but now I was a patient who couldn't find the proper medical terminology to describe my condition. Dr. Skul believed what I was saying and summed it up in her report as follows: "Alice presented with a litany of multi-system symptomatology." Her words summarized in a nutshell the agonizing battle I was facing.

Dr. Skul was conservative in her approach and didn't want to begin unnecessary testing too soon, given the viral nature of my symptoms. So she sent me home with instructions to rest and to call her in a week if things didn't get better. Once home, I called Wandering Wheels to cancel my trip. I was heartbroken. The illusion that I was somehow in control of my life and health had just been shattered.

Re-Routed

My bedridden days blurred into weeks. I had never imagined that one day my health would end and I'd have to struggle to care for my daily needs. But that's precisely what happened, and I was left unsure where my health was from hour to hour. I was unable to predict each night if I would be able to get out of bed the next morning. Forget about being dependable or reliable for work or other commitments. My health scenario reminded me of my first coast-to-coast bicycle trip from Portland, Maine, to Portland, Oregon, in 1977.

"Success is the journey, not the destination" was the trip motto. It was displayed on the follow-up truck and printed on the back of our riding shirts. Prior to the trip, in my youthful excitement at the age of fifteen, I never imagined that biking one hundred miles a day would get hard or become boring. I was too fixated on my newfound cycling freedom and the possibility of making the open road into my expanded playground.

The first leg of the journey was by bus, as Wandering Wheels transported many of us from Upland, Indiana, to Maine. The day after arriving, we began our trip with a ceremony of dipping our rear bicycle wheels into the Atlantic Ocean.

The next task was for all sixty riders to form small groups of six or seven, each with a veteran rider as a team leader. The goal was to find a group with riding compatibility. There I froze, self-conscious and lost in a sea of riders. The sense of security I held as a strong athlete vanished as if it had been an illusion. Carla, an outgoing, friendly group leader and full-time staff member with Wandering Wheels, said, "Hey, come ride with us." Also in that group was Frank, a high school art teacher whom I had enjoyed getting to know on the bus. So I joined them.

Only twelve miles into the trip I faced the rolling terrain of the East Coast. *What have I gotten myself into, thinking I can ride coast-to-coast?* I pondered. I watched the Wandering Wheels bus pass, and the driver waved as he headed back to Indiana. My heart sank. *This trip is for real! I won't see the bus again for forty-two days.* Yikes! I was on the set of wheels that I would roll across the country on. I couldn't imagine the number of pedal revolutions it would take to cycle 3,600 miles. Success had to be the journey, because the destination was unfathomable.

Seeing all the riders in matching attire, our bicycles parked in one place with orange flags rustling in the wind, piqued the locals' curiosity. They would approach us and begin showering us with questions. "What are you doing?

Where did you come from? Where are you going?" Before we'd even started the trip, the answer sounded insane. When the locals heard we were headed to the other side of the country, the common reply was, "Oh, you've got a long way to go!" It was easy to get discouraged by the bystanders' skepticism. However, success was the journey of the present moment.

The trip tested and stretched my physical endurance. There were times when my emotional stamina wavered and I wanted to quit. Riding one hundred miles a day required a mental determination that pushed me to new limits. In that crucible, I learned a reliance on God that I'd never needed before. After completing the trip, I declared with confidence, "If I can bike cross-country, I have the stamina and sheer determination to conquer anything life presents without giving up." Little did I know then what awaited me fifteen years down the road.

Now, in my present state, I was unable to even get out of bed. Only a few days earlier, my typical workday at Rush began at 7 a.m. I would drive an hour through sixteen miles of congested city streets before reaching Englewood, one of the most dangerous, drug-infested neighborhoods in Chicago. There I would make five home health visits to shut-in patients every day. My goal was to leave the area by 2 p.m., before the drug dealers awoke and began doing business again. I'd arrive at Rush's office tense and exhausted from my hyper-attentiveness to the potential dangers on the streets of Englewood. Harried from all the medical paperwork, I never had time to pause and regroup before making follow-up calls, attending meetings, or checking lab reports.

Then I'd head home, hitting Chicago's evening rush hour traffic around 5:30 p.m. My head pounded, my mind raced, and I was trapped at a stress-filled standstill on the interstate, which required all the mental energy I could muster. After getting home, I'd change gears and dash off to my combined social and athletic activities. Afterward, I'd collapse into bed. I would awake the next morning only to repeat the same self-induced hectic schedule. My quiet times were on the fly, if at all.

I thought bicycling coast-to-coast was hard, but it was nothing compared to going from the fast-paced life I knew one day to the sick-bed lifestyle that ruled the next. There were mornings on this medical journey when I thought, *Oh, I feel good*, but soon after getting out of bed I felt like I'd been duped and was utterly drained again.

Awaking every day feeling sick, experiencing debilitating symptoms for at least 85 percent of my waking hours, was a painful and depressing way to live. And yet life went on without my say in the matter. After a night of restless sleep, I would wake up in a zombie-like state. After washing up and eating breakfast, my symptoms were exacerbated to the point that my only goal for the day was survival. I had no option but to cancel my plans for the day and return to bed by 9:30 a.m.

There I would doze for about an hour. At 10:30 a.m. the whole day, and a to-do list a mile long, still loomed on the horizon. I would get up to answer nature's call, begin the dishwasher, and get something to drink. Then I would have no choice but to return to bed. I tried to spend time in "undercover" prayer. I staved off weariness, all the while wondering how useful those prayers were. I didn't feel like I was giving God my best, because I couldn't remember when I'd last felt my best.

I would fall asleep and wake around 2 p.m., hoping I'd feel better. I didn't. My body ached from being in bed. I dragged myself out, trying to ignore the pain and exhaustion. I would gather laundry, empty the dishwasher, or prepare a sandwich for lunch, but by 2:30 p.m. my symptoms would land me back in bed. Heartbroken by my situation and unable to stand the noise of a radio, I would attempt to pray, only to awake at 4:15 p.m. From there I would stumble to my chair to watch the news, in need of the assurance that life was still going on outside.

When I needed social interaction, I'd make a call to Jen, my close friend from nursing school. At the time she had three small children under the age of four, and there was always action in the background. I could tell by the solemn inflection in Jen's voice that she could only talk for a couple of minutes before starting dinner. Jen cared about my situation and could relate to the heartache of a disability since her second oldest son, Nick, had been diagnosed with autism about the same time my medical problem started exhibiting symptoms. Both illnesses were mysterious medical conditions that prompted people to either minimize the suffering or deny there was a problem.

Our parallel paths of suffering drew us even closer as we relied on each other for emotional and spiritual support. While bouncing our fears and struggles of an unknown future off each other, we shared a mutual vulnerability. As nurses, we talked through treatment options prescribed by the medical community, as well as those presented by others outside the medical community. We shared the pain of being ostracized by those we had thought were good friends but who were now unable to step into our messy, unordered worlds.

At the same time, talking with friends like Jen was a glaring reminder that my life had stopped and the world marched on without me. Yet Jen always had enough time to say, "Alice, I'm busy and I don't have much time to talk with you, but it isn't a reflection on our friendship. Even in your discouragement, your life still has a purpose. Your faith is a challenge to me. Thanks for being obedient to God."

As grateful as I was for Jen's comforting words, they weren't enough to penetrate my soul's lament. My desperation found no consolation from the slow-moving clock that now read only 5:30 p.m. I pushed myself to put away my laundry before the debilitating symptoms halted my activity yet again. Unable to bear the thought of going back to bed, I slouched in my chair for the next news segment, which was the same as the first.

By 7 p.m. I was done with dinner. The dirty dishes would remain for another time when I had energy to stand. Then, instead of my body winding down, all of a sudden my biggest spurt of energy came. I felt antsy and bored, and wanted to do something. I would read, write, knit, or play my guitar for a couple of hours, discontented because I was aching to go for a walk or a bicycle ride. My energy tank was on empty. Then I'd bed down for the night around 9 p.m. I was rarely able to spend time outdoors. After experiencing so many of these days, it felt like I was missing entire seasons.

With all this time on my hands, I couldn't help but worry. Unable to work, I faced a predicament: How would I remain financially independent? I was glad that ten months earlier, during my new employee orientation at Rush, I had opted to buy long-term disability insurance for under twenty dollars a month. I certainly hadn't expected I would ever need it! I bought it only because it was cheap and available. Only weeks into my illness, I began the arduous process of applying for short-term disability (STD), long-term disability (LTD), and Social Security disability insurance (SSDI).

Since I had been paying these insurance premiums via automatic paycheck deductions all along, I assumed my coverage was undeniable. I expected it to be easy to claim the benefits now that I was in need. Not so! When I called the Social Security office to get the necessary application forms, the clerk began by saying, "You can expect your paperwork will be denied the first and possibly the second time." Now I faced another burden: How could I fill out the paperwork to justify or prove my disability when the medical professionals didn't have answers or words to articulate what was going on in my body? There was no treatment plan, no objective medical findings, and no one to guide me through the insurance process.

By September 1992, the seventh week of my illness, I wanted answers. But no one had any. So I projected my anger with God onto my physician through a letter. I'm glad I never sent it.

Dear Dr. Skul,

I'm outraged that we've had to build such a relationship. It is unacceptable that my life seems to depend on you and your professional expertise. Developing such a debilitating condition has put my life on hold. I'm grappling with feelings of helplessness, anger, and loss of control. I hurry to specialists' appointments, laboratories for blood draws, and somewhere else for biopsies, scans, and a variety of other medical procedures. My overactive brain runs rampant, conjuring up bizarre diagnoses, as I wait for you to call with the textbook-perfect results.

Health care professionals intrude on my personal space, and there isn't any way to change that reality. My calendar was once filled with work and social engagements. Now it is strewn with medical appointments. I encounter a cold, harsh, sterile world where I'm poked, pricked, and probed, yet no one stops to consider my fear, loneliness, or isolation.

All I want is to get well and resume my life as a participating member of society. I long to rejoin the work force and continue dreaming and pursing the opportunity to lead cycling trips. I beg you, please do something to help me get better.

What I didn't know then was that I would never again rejoin the full-time work force.

A month later, in October, with ever-increasing anxiety, I watched the clock tick by, waiting for a telephone call to inform me that my insurance claim had been approved. By then my $2,500 short-term disability benefits for ten weeks had been paid out. It was less than my monthly salary.

Prior to getting sick, I had planned my financial life to ensure a stable future. It included living frugally, getting an education, putting aside a reserve savings for emergencies, working full-time, and living debt-free. My annual salary at Rush was $36,000 in 1991. According to the average wage index, the average salary in 1991 was $22,000.[iv]

Unable to work, I watched my self-made plans unravel, my reserves dwindle, and my financial security become jeopardized. I worried, *How long can I support myself?* Every time I withdrew money from my savings account I wondered, *When will I hear about LTD or SSDI?*

Making follow-up disability insurance calls was a nightmare. I was told, "We are still waiting for paperwork from your physicians. If we don't hear from them soon, we will make our decision without their input." I'd get off the phone and immediately begin trying to track down the paperwork. But my emergency wasn't anyone else's priority.

In November my illness brought another crisis as I walked out of Rush stripped of my pager, phone, title, and dignity as a respected American citizen. The American dream crumbled for me as my position ended and the permanent state of my disability stormed in.

Such a crisis created ongoing troubles. The day after Christmas, still disillusioned, I wrote in my journal, "There are many areas of stress adding to the feeling of chaos—not having a return date for work, not hearing from LTD, and having my car fail the emissions test. I have medical insurance bills and an increased monthly rent." Frightened, I wondered if my illness would steal my independence, even though I had done everything I could to secure it. How could this have happened to me? My parents had told me I could move back home with them, but in my mind I knew I couldn't go there. I had established myself as an adult, and I wasn't prepared to take that step backward.

January 1993 passed without my disability insurance being approved, and I was confused. February passed, and I was angry. March came, and there were still no insurance answers.

One day in March, on my way to a medical consultation, another bomb dropped when I stopped at my internist's office to pick up an X-ray. Of course, I read the X-ray before giving it to the specialist. Bad idea! Six words jumped off the page at me: "Sarcoma and METS to the bone." Part of me wasn't surprised. The severe pain throughout my body, unaided by the alternating treatment of high doses of anti-inflammatory medications and narcotic pain medications, fit the description of metastasized (METS) bone cancer. Bewildered, I attempted to maintain my composure as my mother and I drove to the appointment.

After the consultation, the specialist promised to call the next day with the results of a CAT scan. That test would give a more decisive answer. But before the day was over, I became my own doctor when I looked in the mirror. My fearful imagination was unable to discern if one of the rolls on my hip was a cancerous tumor or just the leftovers of another bowl of ice cream. From there my emotions spiraled downward. Filled with terror, I planned my funeral. It seemed God was nowhere to be found during that long, restless night. I awoke hopeful to hear from the doctor. But the call never came.

Now I found myself asking the same skeptical questions people had asked me on my coast-to-coast trips. "Where did I come from? Where am I going?" More questions followed. "Lord, am I going to live or die? If I live, do You still have a purpose for my life? How can I become more like You when life has come crashing down?" Hopeless, I questioned, "Where is success amid such a mess?"

The Unknown Road

By April 1993 my hope for relief or a cure was down the drain. After ten months of wandering aimlessly through a daunting medical maze, I had seen nineteen different health care specialists and wasted thousands of dollars on failed treatment options. Two weeks after seeing the latest specialist, I was on edge, waiting to hear whether a CAT scan confirmed cancer. There was still no diagnosis. And even when the diagnosis came, it wouldn't help in finding the solution to my medical catastrophe.

There had been a time when I couldn't wait to change into my cycling gear and take a twenty-mile bike ride after a stressful day at work. I'd push my endurance, trying to break previous time or mileage records. I measured my success through perspiration, muscle fatigue, and a heart rate at 80

percent of maximum. Life as I knew it had ceased to exist, and I could no longer work out my stress in this way. Now a few minutes of exercise resulted in bone-deep pain and an incapacitating brain fog. These relapses left me unable to function, and they could last from one to three days. I could no longer fill my schedule with socializing, volunteering, participating in activities, and going to church. My lifelong coping mechanisms and active lifestyle had been taken from me, and now I was lost.

When I hung up my bike, my family and friends knew my medical situation was serious. They listened to me complain and declare how unfair this battle was, but they also helped me to see that God knew the road I was on.

After those two long weeks passed with no word on the CAT scan, I was at my follow-up appointment with Dr. Skul, my internist, when she became the target of my anxiety explosion. "I need to know! Do I have cancer or not?"

"The CAT scan was clear," she replied. "No cancer." For an instant my anxiety melted away.

Then came the next words out of her mouth: "You have Chronic Fatigue Syndrome/Myalgic Encephalitis (also known as CFS/ME, or CFS).

My fire-engine red face went pale. Terror overcame me.

As a nurse, I knew the word *syndrome* often translates into a "garbage diagnosis." Worse yet, the health care industry is divided on whether CFS is a legitimate diagnosis or the "all-in-your-head syndrome." The media dubs it Yuppie Flu.

Others have the audacity to refer to it as Shirker's Syndrome—as if I'd choose to shirk all my dreams and professional responsibilities for such an unknown prognosis. I thought, *If I had cancer, the doctors would treat me with respect. They'd follow a protocol that would end my symptoms, or cancer would end my life. But this. . . ?*

While CFS isn't terminal, it certainly felt like it as I left Dr. Skul's office. I felt doomed to be a prisoner of CFS, shackled and chained to a myriad of incapacitating symptoms.

Between 1992 and 2003, during the great abyss of my CFS imprisonment, I faced three serious relapses. Each relapse left me more debilitated than the previous one. Once able to work as a nurse, now I could only manage intermittent clerical work. The illness changed the trajectory of my entire life. Everything that was previously familiar became a struggle, leaving me reliably unreliable. My energy was consumed with navigating a myriad of unanswered questions and trying to understand what my anticlimactic diagnosis meant.

Later, two researching physicians would confirm my worst nightmare. "At a congressional briefing (1995), Mark Loveless, M.D., an infectious disease specialist and head of the AIDS and [CFS] Clinic at Oregon Health Sciences University, testified that a [CFS] patient feels every day effectively the same as an AIDS patient feels two months before death."[5] Dr. Nancy Klimas, a leading [CFS] researcher said, "My H.I.V. patients for the most part are hale and hearty thanks to three decades of intense and excellent research and billions of dollars invested. Many of my [CFS] patients, on the other hand, are terribly ill and unable to work or participate in the care of their families. I split my clinical time between the two illnesses, and I can tell you if I had to choose between the two illnesses I would rather have H.I.V (2009)."[6]

Again I was reminded of my bicycle trip through Israel in 1988. I had left for Israel grappling with my faith. I had grown up in a Christian home and accepted Christ at the age of twelve. But at twenty-six, I was at a critical juncture. I had to either commit myself completely to Christ or walk away from my faith altogether. I wasn't content to settle with only giving Him lip service. While I was on the trip, one of my fellow riders named Harvey, a Jewish atheist, said, "Alice, you live your Christian faith." His comment affirmed my faith and helped me to rediscover the reality of my commitment to Christ. Days later, when we came to the Jordan River, I had resolved my soul's internal feud. I celebrated the rededication of my life to the Lord by being baptized there. As my head resurfaced, I said, "God, I will go with You from now on, wherever You lead." I could never have imagined then what that covenant agreement would entail.

Now, four years later, I wondered what life would look like as I followed God through my new diagnosis. The disability insurance process alone seemed insurmountable. The claim application for the benefits I was entitled to—and what my livelihood depended on—included a ten-page questionnaire I had to fill out. One component was to "describe what you do in a typical day." In another section I had to list all the health care providers I'd seen in the last twelve months and the appointment dates for each. By mid-April 1993, ten months after the onset of my illness, I was down to my last dollars when my benefit was finally approved. With this approval I thought all was safe and sound. I was wrong.

For many years the Centers for Disease Control (CDC) stigmatized CFS, not acknowledging it as a valid condition. It wasn't until years later, in June 2000, that the CFIDS Association (another name for CFS) released a news report backing up what I felt at the time. They revealed a financial scandal in which the CDC reallocated millions of dollars away from CFS research. The U.S. General Accountability Office (GAO) later confirmed allegations that the CDC had misallocated funds reserved for CFS research.[7] These negative perceptions of CFS only fueled my insurance battle and left me fearing my daily trip to the mailbox. I would often find an envelope with the dreaded insurance company logo. This would often mean filling out another long questionnaire or jumping through another insurance hoop, when I could barely get out of bed.

From the start of my illness, I was often blindsided by the reactions I got from people. One friend and prayer partner said to me, "Alice, why is your life so hard? Life shouldn't be this hard!" It left me feeling guilty, as if I were somehow responsible for concocting such a life. During midweek church prayer meetings, the group would frequently pray for my health. The following Sunday when the pastor would see me, he would say, "I see God has answered our prayers." His perception, like most, seemed to be, *You look so good.* What he couldn't comprehend was that, although I never lost my healthy appearance, I struggled to walk from my car to the church. The invisible realities of CFS left him and others clueless to the daily battles I faced.

National and international pastors and church leaders, from conservative to charismatic backgrounds, laid hands on me. They anointed me with oil and holy water. They would pray in English, their native language, or in spiritual tongues. I'm sure their prayers were sincere, and I don't doubt that God has the ability to heal. But sometimes it felt like a magic show, with Alice expected to pop out in perfect health. I couldn't help but wonder if some of those "magicians" were more concerned about their own celebrity status than my supernatural healing.

I became wary of letting people pray for me. Prayers all too often came with a high price tag—the expectation that I'd be *healed!* When I didn't cooperate with my part of the transaction and the quick fix failed, I was accused of not having the necessary faith. I've encountered many Christians who are certain that God's plan for my life is complete physical healing. I'm grateful that over time God has led me from a fixation on my physical healing to the greater healing He has provided, and continues to provide—healing of spirit, soul, and mind.

Over the years another challenge for me has been the uncertainty of my ability to function in the warm social milieu of celebrations with family and friends—birthday parties, holidays, funerals, weddings, etc. It's an agonizing, ongoing battle to make the decision between what I want to do and what my health dictates I must do. Prior to any event, I try to imagine it in my head. If the picture is blank beyond my arrival, I have two options. One is to cancel. The other is to push myself beyond my health limitations and participate. But I know what I can expect if I ignore my low energy reading, and I hate taking my medical meltdown show on the road. It begins with an irreconcilable schism between my head and body. They simply stop working together. I lose the brain power required to form cohesive sentences, and my speech becomes gibberish. An intolerance to noise, light, and other sensory stimulation strains my physical capacity. In that compromised state, I have to navigate my way home, risking my life and the lives of others when I get behind the wheel with a delayed reaction time. Once home, I spend at least three days in bed trying to regain enough strength to venture out again.

I learned that before I could listen to my health needs, I first had to let go of what others might expect from me. This required facing the fear of rejection and misunderstanding that could occur from committing to a plan and then not keeping my word. My friends and family have told me, "I always dread the last-minute call from you, because I know what it means." My friend Jen knew how much I loved travel and adventure, and how CFS was squelching that part of me. She said, "I don't understand how you can do something one day, but you can't anticipate or store away energy to come to my house." Unfortunately, my life goes on even though CFS doesn't always let me go along.

Another complex issue I've had to face is summarized by this question that always catches me off guard: "How have you made it through your illness alone?" Up until my mid-twenties, I had never dreamed of falling in love and getting married. I just assumed it was a natural progression in the stages of development. But by thirty I still hadn't found Mr. Right. Dumbfounded, I wondered, *What's wrong with me?* Somehow I attributed my loneliness and discontentment to the "plague" of being single. I believed marriage equated with security, belonging, forever-fulfillment, completeness, and no more lonely nights.

When CFS struck, I experienced the hallmarks of an illness that amplified the feelings of loneliness, isolation, and fear. More than ever I longed to experience the comfort and caress of a marriage partner. My diagnosis left me fearing, *Who will ever want me now? Will my illness steal the gift of love that only a marriage partner can offer?* I tortured myself, thinking life would be easier if I weren't alone. Through a gradual process over several years, as God met my every need, I came to realize that only God was able to care for all my needs. I clung to the hope that He would keep His promise: "I will never leave you nor forsake you."[8]

I had some friends who had long since tired of my arduous medical journey, and it was difficult to see these friendships end. I knew the challenges of an illness like mine could not only destroy friendships but also leave marriage partners feeling like total strangers, unable to find the comfort and intimacy they once knew. My situation could have been worse, I realized. I couldn't imagine myself trying to care for my own needs while also fulfilling the duties of a wife and a mother.

The demands of my illness forced me to find a support network to help me navigate my health challenges. I didn't find an established CFS support group in my area that was a good fit, so I had to invest in building my own support system. Betty, a friend who was in her seventies, was an important member of my team. When we met to play games, eat pizza, and pray together, I took the risk and shared those raw, trapped emotions that left me feeling like damaged goods. Betty's first husband had died, leaving her single for the first time in forty years. She had recently remarried but she knew the joys and challenges that came with being single. As we shared, I began to recognize the freedom encompassed by the God-given gift of singleness. The liberty to accept or reject social invitations without impacting a spouse is priceless. I realized that being on my own gave me the autonomy to build a personal social network in a way I wouldn't have been able to as a married person.

My medical issues continued. In 1996 I experienced another relapse and my heart rate went wild again, so Dr. Skul ordered a tilt table test to try to diagnose my problem. The test involved changing positions in order to evaluate my abnormally fast heart rate. Within thirty seconds the EKG machine began beeping with an ever-quickening frequency as my heart rate went from 90 to 160 beats per minute. Over the next twenty-eight minutes, as I remained in the upright standing position, my heart rate remained high, while my blood pressure remained normal. This was a medical conundrum. My face and neck turned flaming red. I felt dizzy, nauseous, and weak.

The abnormality from the tilt table test provided a measurable marker, which gave credibility to an otherwise elusive condition. It now made sense why walking two flights of stairs to my third-floor apartment or just standing still was impossible at times. This objective medical finding flustered physicians for years as they tried to understand and treat my specific case. After the test they prescribed medication for me, but it came with adverse effects. It slowed my heart rate to the point where I couldn't even get out of bed. As a result

I couldn't live alone. I shared a house with two housemates, still longing to find a way to live a somewhat normal life.

Weeks later the side effects of this medication landed me in the emergency room with a severe asthma attack. By then I'd had it. The result of this visit sent me out looking for answers again. Surely someone had the solution I was looking for. The next stop was an endocrinologist. During our initial phone conversation he asked, "Are you a wall stander—always supporting yourself against a wall when you stand? Are you unable to stand still—are you always fidgeting? When you stand still, do your feet turn purple? Does your heart race? Do you have to avoid the sun when the temperature is above seventy-six degrees? When you shower, does the hot water make you feel faint? Are your showers quick?" I answered, yes to all of the above.

I was shocked that he could name symptoms I had never articulated before. He prescribed a new treatment plan from Johns Hopkins University. I was required to take an eleven-pill-a-day medication cocktail that caused me to gain twenty pounds over a short period of time. It wasn't the ideal long-term plan, but it was the best so far.

Thanks to CFS, I felt like an outcast at church, a guinea pig at my physician's office, and a burden even to my friends. My medical condition left me sidelined, having to cancel commitments and appearing to friends and acquaintances as if I no longer valued our time together. It hurt deeply to know my actions were portraying a false impression of unreliability and unconcern. Nothing could have been further from the truth. I shudder to think of where I would have been—or where I'd be today—without my support system.

With their help, I began to see that maybe my struggles, like Job's, weren't all about me. The following quote, which I found around 1997, seemed to summarize my life. It hangs on my bathroom wall as a reminder that God is still in charge.

> *I am leading my child to the heavenly land.*
> *I am guiding her day by day,*
> *and I ask her now as I take her hand*
> *to come home by a rugged way.*
> *It is not a way she herself would choose.*
> *For its beauty she cannot see,*
> *but she knows not what her soul would lose*
> *if she trod not this path with me.*[9]
> —Anonymous

There were times when it was a struggle to keep CFS from stealing my identity. I remember distinctly October 6, 1997, when my pastor prayed for me. Afterward he shared with me, "The picture God has given me is one where your life is like a top. The string is tightly wound up, but it isn't engaged yet." His words struck me. I had no idea how to engage the string with the top in my life. That night I wrote the following prayer: "God, will You give me an enjoyable position where I have variety in my work, utilizing my interests, talents, and education—one that would envelop my love for Christ into a God-size position?"

Now in 2003, twelve years since the onset of my lonely journey into the great abyss of CFS, there were still no answers or solutions. I couldn't believe it! Would medicine ever make advances that would help explain this mysterious illness? I wondered if I would ever find an escape from this great abyss. Even though the road was hard, I kept the pact I'd made with my Lord at the Jordan River in 1988—to never again ask the question, "God, are You worth living for?"

5

An Uphill Climb

As my health limitations from CFS continued to increase, the walls of disability and disappointment caved in on me. My financial security collapsed. Despair paralyzed me, and I began to wonder if quitting was an option. But my God remained steadfast.

During this time I remembered the commitment I had made in 1988. Days after I was baptized in the Jordan River, we passed the Dead Sea, the lowest place on earth at 1,312 feet below sea level. I looked toward the western edge of the desert where Masada ("fortress" in Hebrew) towered 1,476 feet above the Dead Sea.

One book about the climb offers this warning: "If you are a hearty soul (or think you are) [then you] climb Masada from the east." Such a climb can cause "an unusual strain on body muscles which have remained dormant since the last time you tried a fool thing like this."[10] But I was up for the challenge. Bike over my shoulder, I climbed the twelve hundred feet, up eighty steps, over the two-mile-long Snake Path, and then down the other side, where I began riding again. I was certainly feeling those dormant muscles!

Snake Path was filled with sharp curves and protruding rocks. I feared losing my footing and having my bicycle fall on me, causing me to tumble backward. As I approached the halfway point, the wind began blowing and it started raining. By the time I reached the peak, I was chilled to the bone from the drop in temperature, and a chill of a different kind had overcome my soul.

I couldn't imagine how the same panoramic view that exhilarated me could have left 960 Jews in the first century horrified and hopeless. But what those Jews had seen from Masada was the Roman army, which was about to overtake them. The attack had blindsided them, and they had all chosen suicide rather than succumb to their enemy.[11] Choked with emotion, my Jewish friend Harv spoke the short Israeli oath of determination, which military cadets make there. "Never forget. Never again." For me, Masada was the spiritual fortress where I solidified the allegiance I made in the Jordan River. *Alice, never forget God. Never again.*

Knowing that suicide is the number one killer of CFS patients made my spiritual Masada even more important. Dr. David McKay, a clinical psychologist and professor at Trinity Seminary, helped me to navigate the sharp edges of grief, loss, and altered self-image on the dark road of my illness. As time went by, psychological help wasn't enough. Whenever I experienced another physical relapse, my emotions began to unravel. My outward appearance was one of strength and health, but I was unable to regain my internal balance. Finally, at a 1996 appointment with the endocrinologist, he said, "There is more to life than a good heart rate and healthy blood pressure. I think it's time for an antidepressant and anti-anxiety medication. By the time you've come to this point with CFS and tachycardia [elevated heart rate], you have been through Hell."[12] The orders to see a psychiatrist caused me to ache with still another type of pain.

I made the appointment, but in the days leading up to it I frequently called my friend Jen for comfort. I had no idea what I needed, but Jen recognized that I was in an emotional crisis, and she spoke truth into my life. "Alice, you need help *now*. When we hang up, you must call Dr. Skul and get medication. Report back to me after talking to her." Before hanging up, Jen prayed for me. She was hoping for me when I no longer had it in me to hope for myself. My physician got me the help I needed to make it through the next several days until my appointment with the psychiatrist.

When I saw the psychiatrist, he ordered an antidepressant and anti-anxiety medication. I needed help, so I took the medication. But it wasn't as easy to overcome the internal tapes blaring in my head about the stigma connected with taking such medications. That battle raged for months before a friend confronted me on this issue. "You are accepting when others need psychotropic medications. As a nurse, you've encouraged patients to seek the same help from their doctors. People who need medication for depression are just like people who need insulin for diabetes." Ouch. The truth hurt. I was left to work through my repulsion and the false pride in my heart.

Another serious predicament that accompanied my disability was the added financial challenge. I dreaded the question, "What do you do for a living?" It stumped me. *Um, my profession is CFS disability? My job description includes seeing doctors, taking drugs, dealing with insurance companies, experiencing disappointments, and attempting to protect myself from financial crises.* I'd tell them, "I live off a trust fund. My Father 'owns the cattle on a thousand hills.'"[13] But that response only provoked more questions. What they really wanted to know was, "How do you support yourself financially?"

When I was employed, it had been easy to link my value, purpose, dignity, worth, security, and status to my professional identity as a nurse. But now, when answering these questions, I felt as if people switched on their brain calculators to determine my net worth. I sensed they were taking the liberty to determine whether I was a valued asset to society or a worthless liability that should be wiped off the books. Maybe my fear was directly linked to having once judged other people in this way. When this degrading conclusion was made about me, the emotional impact left me smoldering.

Needless to say, the combination of medical disability and financial challenge impacted my relationships, and sometimes they had to be redefined. My dad often said, "There isn't anything harder than watching your child suffer. I wish there was something I could do to help." I was certainly in need of help. I knew my family had managed their finances well, which left them in a position to offer assistance. I also knew Scripture says, "If anyone does not provide for his relatives, and especially for members of his household, he has denied the faith and is worse than an unbeliever."[14]

My part was to let them help, and while I was grateful, I was also afraid that accepting their aid would infringe on my autonomy. After wrestling through that tension for some time, I eventually asked my parents if they would cover my monthly medical insurance premiums. It was a way they could lighten my financial responsibilities within clear boundaries, allowing me to maintain my dignity and independence. Others helped as well. My cousin, a dentist, assumed care for my dental needs, and a family friend who is an accountant does my taxes free of charge.

Another complication created by my disability was a spotty work history. Employment gaps, along with my medical restrictions, made securing a job nearly impossible. I thought the Americans with Disabilities Act protected someone struck by illness. If not, then the Family and Medical Leave Act would ensure my rights. While this act states, "Most employees must be restored to their original or equivalent positions with equivalent pay, benefits, and other employment terms,"[15] it also contains conditions that are open to interpretation by employers. Apparently my case was one of the exceptions.

When I tried to get my job back at Rush, ten months after my initial illness, it didn't happen. They said, "There aren't any nursing positions throughout the entire hospital system that could accommodate your twelve-hour-a-week medical limitation." I was left feeling the sting of discrimination.

Yet another stressor was the constant uncertainty that accompanied my disability insurance. On July 19, 2002, I received a haunting letter from the company: "Please be advised that we have started a review of your claim." I didn't know the letter was a red flag. But four months later, on December 4, 2002, I got a follow-up call. "I will be in the area on December 12, 2002," the insurance representative stated. "I would like to come by your home to talk with you." I didn't want him in my home; instead, we met at the public library.

During the week preceding the interview, nervousness and sheer terror, created a pit in my stomach. I had no idea what this was about, but I suspected it wasn't good. The night before the appointment, Ellen, an acquaintance from church, heard about my meeting. She prayed for me, then offered to go with me to the interview. What a relief to know I wasn't going alone.

At the appointment Ellen sat opposite from me so I could see her. She had her head in a magazine, but she heard everything. When the man began speaking, the words *insurance investigator* hit me as if I'd just been shot with a round of ammunition. Was I on trial? If so, for what? He showed me his identification, and he asked to see my driver's license. Then he delved into a thorough investigation. He asked about my medical history, treating physicians, medications, treatments, work history, restrictions, limitations, and activities.

Then he stated, "Now I have a video to show you." For four days that November, a private investigation company had followed me with a surveillance camera. When I heard that, I was unable to contain my anger. It was a violation that left me feeling degraded, stripped of my dignity. The written report read,

Thursday, November 7, 2002

5:45 p.m. Arrive at the subject's residence. The subject is standing in the front room of the house with the front curtains open.

Friday, November 8, 2002

7:32 a.m. Video. Spot check subject residence upon arrival. . . . No subject activity observed.

7:48 a.m. Established a direct surveillance position next door. There is a four-foot high fence. . . . The subject's residence is in open view from the street.

7:54 a.m. The investigator contacts the Wheaton police department.

11:06 a.m. Video. The subject exits the driveway. . . . Begin mobile surveillance.

2:07 p.m. Video. An unidentified male riding a bicycle enters the subject's property and walks to the residence. The view is blocked, and no subject activity is observed.

2:33 p.m. Video. The unidentified male exits the residence and walks with his bike down the street.

2:56 p.m. Video of the subject as she exits the residence and begins raking leaves.

The written summary of the video focused on my ability to perform normal activities without any "visible physical signs of discomfort."

As the video played, I felt vilified, demoralized, and dehumanized simply for trying to live my life. Afterward, on the drive home, Ellen said, "You did a great job. You were honest, and you have nothing to feel ashamed about. That was terrible, even for me to watch."

The next day I prayed, "May it be true of my life that the more it is scrutinized, the more it becomes a mystery where You alone are the only answer." Five weeks later my friend Jen said, "It seems like hardships keep coming and trying to erode your core of contentment."

During this time I cried out to God. Here is one of the prayers I wrote: "Pain, trials, and hardships were part of the life You went through. I know I will go through them too, as You prepare me for the part I am to have in Your mighty, sovereign plan of furthering Your Kingdom work. I want to lift high Your cross through my suffering."

The very next day I received notice from the insurance company that a mandatory, non-biased, third party medical examination with a neurologist had been scheduled. The insurance company picked the physician, scheduled the appointment, and paid for it.

When the day of the examination arrived, my friend and former nursing school instructor drove me to the appointment. She was also present during the examination. As the physician entered the room, I froze. He tried to appear friendly, but his demeanor showed his suspicion of my condition. I despised the fact that all I had on was a hospital gown. I was now about to experience physical exploitation in the name of medicine. To keep my disability insurance, I had to allow a stranger to touch me, knowing he didn't have my best interests in mind.

The written report from my own doctor referenced my low-grade fevers and tachycardia, but this doctor didn't check either of those during the exam. His entire evaluation was irrelevant to my condition, since there are no clear medical markers for CFS. Yet the doctor's word held power over mine.

He wrote, "The patient is well appearing and in a mild amount of distress. . . . somewhat emotionally labile, and on the verge of tears. . . . Ms. Teisan may have mild psychological impairment; however, she does not have any organic pathological basis for disability." I left part two of the interview irate, with another intimate layer of my privacy assaulted.

Six weeks passed, and on April 2, 2003, the gauntlet dropped. I read the following words: "Your claim has been terminated as of February 14, 2003." (This was the same date I had seen the insurance-chosen neurologist.) My heart plummeted to a new depth of despair. Then I read, "An overpayment has occurred in the amount of $1,197."

Questions erupted from deep within. How could they discontinue my benefits, guaranteed to me until I was sixty-five? I was only forty-one! And now they wanted back payment? Could God still care for me now that I was poor in spirit, health, and income? I was making only $450 a month working in my cousin's dental office. I was terrified. I cried, "God, if insurance isn't how You plan to provide for my needs, You'll have to figure out another way to care for me!"

As I called my friends and family, all they could say was, "I'm sorry. I'll pray for you." I believed in prayer, but at that juncture the word sounded hollow to hear and even harder to do. But I persisted, and on Good Friday I wrote out the following verse. "Therefore, since we have been made right in God's sight by faith, we have peace with God because of what Jesus Christ our Lord has done for us."[16]

When I couldn't feel God's peace, I clung to His promise. I longed for a character-building confidence in Christ to emerge from my crisis, not an embittered fixation on my unjust circumstances. As I prayed, I acknowledged,

"My insurance trial is not an accident but an appointment in Your eternal plan, just as Jesus' death was an appointment in God's plan." I went on to journal, "While others look at my health and disability trials, may they ask the question, 'Who is her God?' I long for the answer to appear through my countenance as the glory of God radiates through my life."

There was still the issue of the overpayment to insurance. In need of ending this horrendous chapter of my life, I decided to pay the money back. I wasn't about to allow the insurance company to exploit me again by marring my excellent credit rating.

How ironic that only a month after the insurance company deemed me no longer disabled, Ben, my three-year-old nephew, came into my bedroom in great distress. His shoulders slouched, and a frown covered his face. Cautiously, he moved toward my bed.

With a trembling voice, Ben blurted out, "Aunt Alice, why are you always sick? When are you going to get better?"

I replied, "Ben, Aunt Alice's sickness is not going to make her die."

A smile came across Ben's face. He jumped into my bed, gave me a big hug, and said, "I love you!"

My nephew's words did more than any report could do to affirm that this condition wasn't all in my head.

With doors closing for steady income and insurance, it was time to get creative. Finding ways to live below my means—once a hobby—was now a necessity if I hoped to remain financially solvent. Regardless of the unsettling financial blows that assaulted me, I had to continue taking the next steps and overcoming fears so CFS didn't rob me of living a full life. But it made me wonder, *How am I making it?* I decided to keep track of the ways God was providing through a "God-come" ledger.

One day my cousin said, "I have $800 in plane vouchers we can't use. Would you like them?"

The next time I saw Dr. Skul, she asked, "How are you making it financially?"

I said, "I earn $450 monthly and live off a promise: 'My God will supply every need of [mine] according to his riches in glory in Christ Jesus.'"[17]

She said, "Your faith is what has seen you through your illness. Nothing I've prescribed or done has given you the strength."

Her words confirmed that she was watching my life and that, indeed, God was the Victor.

Before the appointment ended, I asked Dr. Skul for some medication samples. The supply shelf was empty, but the office manager said, "The drug representative is standing right here. If you sign for the medication, Alice can have all the samples she needs!"

"Praise the Lord," I proclaimed.

Another day I saw a chiropractor. "Did you know the doctor wrote 'no charge' for today's visit?" asked the office staff.

Only hours later, and again consumed by my financial worries, I opened a letter and a check fell out. A cousin wrote, "Thanks for helping in our time of need. We'd now like to help in yours."

Later that same afternoon, I got a train ticket using an unexpected free ride voucher. God was astounding me with His miracles.

While experiencing God's simple yet profound provisions, my relationship with Him was growing more intimate. *Now I need a black shoe mat*, I thought. About a week later I prayed, "Lord, I need to hear from you today." Looking out my living room window, I saw something black on my front lawn. I was aggravated, thinking it was another piece of trash thrown out of a car window. What I discovered was that God had made an unexpected drive-by delivery of a new black shoe mat. All I could do was acknowledge that, indeed, "Yours, O LORD, is the greatness and the power and the glory and the victory and the majesty, for all that is in the heavens and in the earth is yours."[18]

The Lord continued to surprise me. One day I asked a friend, "Will you join me for a Chicago Cubs baseball game sometime this spring?" Afterwards I worried, *How can I afford this?* Two days later she called back and said, "What are you doing on April 23? My mom just won four tickets to the Cubs game. I can't use them. Would you like them?" Shocked, I exclaimed, "Yes! It's my birthday. What an awesome way to celebrate!" I never stopped to think that the Lord cared so much about me that He would throw such a fun birthday party, just for me.

On another occasion my neighbor was cutting a huge limb off a tree. I asked, "Would you cut the wood up so I can use it for firewood? I've been praying for firewood." Afterwards he said, "Watching God answer your prayers has challenged me to pray for what I need also."

My expectation to see God didn't always happen as I anticipated. One day I received a free health care visit. I was grateful. However, when I returned to the same provider next time I was expecting God to provide another free visit. But it didn't happen. I learned that God's part is deciding how He will provide. My part is to graciously acknowledge His provision as a gift.

While I was recounting how God had provided for me, a church leader asked, "Are you aware that many people never get anything free?" I wasn't. This "God-come" exercise taught me that our miracle-working God wants the glory for providing our every need. Over a six-month period my "God-come" total was $11,900, from more than forty sources, which exceeded what my insurance would have paid out. Through that exercise I came to see my faulty thinking. I thought God needed my finances, something to work with, before He could provide my needs. I had to confess that I had mistaken the God of money for the Almighty God. All I could do was trust that through the process, God would somehow build my soul's investment portfolio.

One day while praying, I sensed God saying "I have something big for you to do, but you aren't ready yet." So I asked Him to make me ready. The next day I was enjoying an outing with a friend. Since we had both just bought a house, I asked, "How did you qualify for a loan?"

She replied, "I paid cash for my home." Suddenly, my pleasant spirit was drowned out by an unexpected foul attitude.

Later, when I got home, I took the thirty-one-inch cross down off my bedroom wall and clung to it during prayer. "Lord, I don't know what happened today, but please shine Your light on my foul mood." He did. I was reminded of my desire from seven years earlier to live the rest of my life debt free. Now I was strapped by a thirty-year mortgage, fretting and wondering, *Will I be able to afford my house in the future, on a fixed income?* The turmoil inside gave me a glimpse of what the Bible means when it says, "The rich rules over the poor, and the borrower is the slave of the lender."[19] I sensed the Lord saying, "I've made it possible for you to own your home. Now, Alice, you must be willing to pay the price for your desire, as I did by going to the cross for your sins." At first I wrote off the idea, because it felt like an insurmountable task.

Over the four months since buying my home, the financial markets were approaching some of the highest levels experienced in the 1990s. I thought my investments had grown to the point where I had enough money to pay off my home, while still leaving $10,000 in savings. But I didn't know how to determine the cost in capital gain taxes and investment broker fees to cash in my investments. I had never shared my finances with people outside my family, and I didn't want my family's input now for fear it would sway my decision.

Thus, it forced me to share my finances with others. The idea stirred paranoia, unfounded fears of being critiqued and criticized. Uncertain how to proceed in taking the radical step of obedience, I sought counsel from a church leader. She said, "The way you handle your finances is a talent the Lord has given you. You have been faithful with a little, and He has multiplied it for you." She encouraged me to talk with the financial officer of the church.

Proceeding forward was a process. After talking with him, I still had to deal with my fears. What would happen if I needed money in the future and didn't have any? By paying off my home, I was cashing in the security of my financial portfolio. There, I was convicted of how I had allowed my financial portfolio to become an idol. Before I could proceed, I had to confess the sin of idolatry and invite God in to clean up that area of my life.

Within a month of talking with the church financial officer, I proceeded by writing out my fourth and final house payment. It was there that my life began to take a major turn, securing my future and allowing me to follow Him in reckless abandonment on the mysterious journey that lay ahead. What a relief it would be four years later not to have a mortgage when my insurance payments ended.

Through the discernment process of paying off my home, God uncovered my financial abilities to the church. Only months later the church leadership asked me to head up the benevolence committee. I felt weak and worn down from living seven years with CFS. I perceived myself as disabled, but the leadership stressed that I was a pillar of strength, and a valued member of the congregation. The invitation to serve gave me the opportunity to focus on something outside myself that encompassed many of my strengths.

The words of Jesus to Simon felt true of me, too. "Simon, Simon, behold, Satan demanded to have you, that he might sift you like wheat, but I have prayed for you that your faith may not fail. And when you have turned again, strengthen your brothers."[20] Here was my opportunity to do the same.

While serving, my committee members helped me learn to integrate the unpredictable nature of my health issues into a team setting. The benevolence committee was the precursor, a dry run for initiating the ministry God had for me, which He would unveil six years later. With my illness, I never knew if I could get out of bed, but one thing I would always do was serve the Lord as part of my spiritual life.

As my limitations increased, and I found myself in this relentless CFS battle, I was glad God had won the war for my soul's allegiance at Masada. Now, like never before, I had to continue turning my eyes toward the Lord, admitting all my raw emotions, and clinging to His promise. "Trust in the LORD with all your heart, and do not lean on your own understanding. In all your ways acknowledge him, and he will make straight your paths."[21]

6

Fuel for the Future

In September 2003, Ellen, my friend from church who had joined me for the insurance interrogation, asked, "Would you join Walt and me for dinner today after church? We are having a Wheaton College graduate student and his wife over for dinner. John and Carolyn Lutembeka are from Tanzania." When I accepted the invitation, I didn't anticipate the role Ellen and Walt's hospitality would have in God's plan for my life. But it was, indeed, a divinely orchestrated gathering.

During dinner I sat next to John, and we became engrossed in conversation about his ministry in Tanzania. As I was leaving, I sensed that God wanted me to invite the Lutembekas over for dinner one day soon. But I was having trouble connecting the dots. At first I thought I'd misheard Him.

What do I have to give at this point in my life? I contemplated. There I was, still battling the insurance nightmare after five long months. As if it weren't enough to deal with the termination of my long-term disability insurance, only two days earlier, Social Security disability insurance denied yet another claim for coverage. I was bewildered. How could God ask me to reach out to others when my self-esteem was low, my self-doubts raged, and my spirit was broken?

My excuses mounted. Six weeks later I wrote in my prayer journal, "I have no strength, no appetite. Lord, I'm hanging by a thread." My mind wasn't on entertaining, yet the nudges from God persisted. Would God really ask me to give when I felt so bad? "I don't have anything to offer them. Furthermore, they wouldn't want to come!" I declared.

I allowed my feelings, logic, financial state, and circumstances to take over my thinking. I hadn't considered that maybe the Lutembekas were God's special message carriers. Then one night I was reading a book about a woman who was living her dream. I said, "Lord, all the good ideas are gone!" I had no idea at the time how God would use the Lutembekas to prove that idea false.

The next day when I saw Carolyn Lutembeka at church, I knew I could no longer ignore God's nudging. I asked her, "Would you and your husband join me for dinner tonight?" With delight, they accepted the invitation.

Minutes after our church service began, I felt so sick I had to leave. I knew the routine. I had no choice but to go home to bed. Once there I fretted, "How can I entertain tonight? My house is a shambles, I don't have a menu planned, and I'm low on food." But I had to let those thoughts go so I could rest my weary body for the next three hours. I awoke feeling anything but rested—more like a truck had plowed me over. I was left with an incapacitating brain fog. But there was no turning back. Now more than ever, I wondered how anything good could come from our time together.

Within minutes of the Lutembekas' arrival, they showed their curiosity and comfort level by asking many questions. "How much do you pay for rent?" came first.

"I own my house."

Next came, "How much is your mortgage?"

I said, "I don't have a mortgage." Then I proceeded to tell them the story of paying off my home.

Trying to figure things out, John continued, "How much do you make?"

"Four hundred and fifty dollars a month."

A shocked expression flashed across their faces. "Oh, you can't live on that in America!" they said. "Wow, you are a woman of faith."

Adding to their shock was the cultural mystery of a single female owning a home and living alone. In Tanzania, women typically live with their families until marriage. In their society, to an even greater extent than in the United States, owning a home is associated with being a "real adult" and linked to the rite of passage gained through marriage.

After dinner I was ready to ask them my own list of questions. But I didn't get past my first question: "How can our church help your ministry in Tanzania?"

John replied, "If every family in the church gave a $100 gift, each gift would buy a new bicycle, allowing a traveling evangelist to reach five villages. The distance from village to village can equal a six-hour walk." They continued talking, but that was all I heard.

Bikes . . . Africa . . . bikes. The words kept replaying in my head. At the same time a holy arrow pierced my heart.

This couple had no idea that bikes were woven into the matrix of my life. Maybe there were still good ideas left—and maybe God had one set aside just for me. In that moment my brain began buzzing. The turbo-rewind button of my life was set in motion, and in an instant it rewound back twenty-some years to my junior high days. Was it possible that God had a plan to weave even a horrific experience from my childhood into His spectacular masterpiece for my life?

On a cold January morning, in the middle of my eighth grade year, I was filled with resentment and angst as I was ordered to take a different route to a different school. It was the result of a federal law over the desegregation issue that had been brewing throughout the country since the 1950s.

Instead of the one-mile bike ride to Arthur, the neighborhood school I had attended my first semester, I was now rerouted to a bus stop a block from home. About twenty other classmates and I boarded a yellow school bus there, headed to our first day at Joy Junior High, another school in Detroit.

I wasn't prepared for what awaited us after the bus door closed. The driver began barking orders: "Sit in your seats, no loud talking, no pushing, no fighting, no . . ." We drove south on Outer Drive before turning west on Chandler Park Drive. By the time we turned south on St. Jean Street, we had entered the bombed-out area of Detroit's East Side, affected by the riots of 1967. By the time we were within a mile of our new school, I felt like we were heading into another country. I spotted cars resting on blocks where tires once were and a pool of shattered glass that had once represented a car's window.

The school grounds were littered with potato chip wrappers and empty liquor bottles. The landscape was covered in mud where there had once been grass. The bushes were unkempt and infested with weeds. The school building was a drab gray color. I'd seen these sights before, from a car window. But I wasn't prepared for the feeling of disgrace and revolt that welled up inside knowing it was where I'd have to go to school for the next twenty-three weeks.

A guard resembling a gang ringleader welcomed us through an entrance that seemed fit for criminals who were being escorted to jail. The hallways were grungy and unruly, filled with screaming, shoving, and fighting. It was a stark contrast to the laughter-filled halls at Arthur. I felt as if I'd been thrown into a den of starving lions.

The awkwardness of being at a new school, where I knew I wasn't wanted and where I didn't want to be, left me in a fury of emotions. What I remember most about the first day was the debriefing session with my friends on the bus ride home. From our conversation I learned that the playground/outdoor gym field was called Death Valley, a near literal interpretation for one of my friends. He had a swollen eye and other injuries as his medals of survival, along with a guarantee that his days at Joy were over.

By the end of the first week, only three of us from the initial twenty continued to board the bus. Critics said, "In a phenomenon dubbed *white flight*, many transferred their children to private schools or simply moved to suburbs where few, if any, nonwhites lived."[22] Even though I had cried and pleaded with my folks to transfer me to a private school, it was to no avail. Both my parents were Detroit public school teachers at schools in close proximity to Joy. Their rationale was, "We can't run from trouble. We must face it and make the most of the situation. God will protect us." I felt like I had no options left. I had an overload of bad experiences and no means to process them.

The apathy on the part of many of the teachers and administrators was something I'd never experienced before. The law could order students to change schools, but it was powerless over changing the hearts and attitudes of parents, and teachers who weren't in agreement with the plan.

During my time at Joy, I experienced bullying on a whole new level. One day students made a human barricade across the hallway when school was dismissed so I couldn't get to my bus. When the bus driver was ready to leave, my brother wouldn't let her. Instead, he and a newfound African-American friend went looking for me. When those forming the barricade saw Dan's friend, an icon of gang power, they let me go. Another day students put gum on my chair and then watched me return and sit on it. How humiliating to my adolescent ego. Then there was the time someone gave me a friendly pat on my back. Unbeknownst to me, he had ink all over his hand. When I looked in the mirror after showering that night, I saw the ink smeared on my back. It had ruined my brand-new blouse, and it created another layer of wreckage to my heart.

In an attempt to stave off the bullying, I tried to make myself invisible. I skipped gym class for the entire semester by hiding out in Mrs. Smith's music room and playing my violin. I tried hiding my intelligence by rarely studying. It didn't work.

In the midst of this mess I also faced a spiritual predicament. Ten months prior to going to Joy Junior High, I had decided to make the faith of my parents my own by accepting Christ as my Savior. The verse God gave me for the next chapter of my life was, "Do you not know that in a race all the runners run, but only one receives the prize? So run that you may obtain it."[23]

I couldn't understand that verse within the context of my present reality. The failed desegregation project, meant for the bettering of society, left me emotionally bloodied. I battled with my ransacked emotions for years, all the while wondering, *What is wrong with me? Why did I once have so many friends and now I'm lonely and depressed and feel like an outcast? What am I to do about the deep-seated prejudice that has taken root in my heart as a result of my pain?* I knew it saddened God's heart, because His word says, "You have heard that it was said, 'You shall love your neighbor and hate your enemy.' But I say to you, Love your enemies and pray for those who persecute you."[24] I had prayed for those who hurt me, but it didn't change my feelings.

I wanted to run to receive the prize, but I hated my African-American classmates. As the years progressed, I needed help working through my anger, depression, and prejudice. I couldn't imagine finding my way out of the dark hole that semester at Joy Junior High School created in me. I didn't know then that it would take more than twenty years of hard work, prayer, and forgiveness to heal my heart of the battle wounds from that semester.

After resurfacing from that memory and regrouping, I refilled the Lutembekas teacups and I interjected a few lines into the conversation. By then two hours had flown by. The Lutembekas suggested we pray, the African way of ending time together.

After saying good-bye to the Lutembekas, I got ready for bed and paused for what I thought was a bedtime prayer. However, even though I was bone tired, the night was just beginning. God challenged me to give $1,200, the cost of my Schwinn Paramount, to buy bicycles for pastors in Tanzania. Even though I had practiced sacrificial giving in the past, a three-hour wrestling match still ensued. I wondered again if I'd heard God right. The idea seemed ludicrous. Fear welled up inside me over the fact that I was only making $450 a month and I couldn't forecast my health or financial future.

My first prayer was, "Lord, forgive me for having taken three months to respond and invite the Lutembekas over." Then I thanked God for His patience and ended with, "Help me to obey faster in the future." If I had delayed seven days longer, the Lutembekas would have returned to Tanzania permanently. I realized God wasn't asking if I felt like obeying Him, nor was He asking me to understand everything ahead of time. He just wanted me to trust His wisdom and obey His directions in the daily events of life.

As I continued praying, the words *bikes* and *Africa* reminded me of a trip I had taken twenty years earlier. The strong desire to go to Zimbabwe, Africa, in 1983 was born out of my Joy Junior High experience seven years earlier. The movie *Roots*, based on the novel by Alex Haley, aired the semester I was at Joy. It sent many of my classmates on a search for their roots. I, too, wanted to see the roots some of my African-American classmates had talked about reintegrating into their lives.

The nine-week summer mission project with The Evangelical Alliance Mission (TEAM) took place between my junior and senior years of nursing school. Once we were in Zimbabwe, the plan was for me to work as a nurse in a bush clinic, where I would have the opportunity to experience medical missions as I considered God's plan for my future.

Instead, when I got to Harare, Zimbabwe, I found there had been a change of plans. There were no other medical personnel at the bush clinic, and TEAM didn't feel it was wise for me, still a nursing student, to go there alone. Instead, I was loaned to Scripture Union and Youth for Christ for the summer. The two organizations shared an office in Harare. There I was assigned to secretarial work.

During those nine weeks I lived with the Nyatsambos, a family of five. Tobias was a pastor, and his wife, Rose, was a schoolteacher. Their three young children were in elementary school. The Nyatsambos welcomed me in as part of their family. I participated in their extended family gatherings, where they shared meals by eating out of a common bowl. The older generation only spoke Shona, so my cultural blunders probably offered fodder for their entertainment. Their contagious laughter was the only invitation I needed. I joined in, laughing right along with them.

Since we all went in different directions each morning, I used the men's-style family bike for my six-mile round trip to the office. The cultural norm for women was to wear skirts, even when biking. That was a first for me. Even mounting the bike—slanting it and lowering the bar to step over—was a challenge. Once I'd successfully mounted the cheaply made bike, the next test was cycling with a broken brake cable. Each time I rode the bike I thought, *If only I had a cable and the right tool, I could fix this bicycle.* I didn't have either, nor could I buy them anywhere.

While I lived with the Nyatsambos, we engaged in many discussions about culture and missions. One such discussion occurred the morning after I returned from a trip to the bush clinic on a small missionary plane. I'd had the opportunity to attend the opening ceremony of this new clinic, and the locals showered me with attention. At breakfast Tobias asked if it was fair for me, an American, to get more fanfare than the local government official, who had walked to the ceremony.

With my brilliant twenty-one-year-old knowledge base, I proceeded to say, "Due to the political unrest, if I hadn't flown there, I couldn't have gone."

He said, "Did you ever consider that maybe you shouldn't have gone?"

No, I hadn't! His question rocked my egocentric world and provided my first conundrum related to the complexities of cross-cultural ministry.

The insights I gleaned in Zimbabwe that summer were all part of my reconciliation process. God was softening my heart. The people I met in Zimbabwe were hard workers. Even though life was harsh for many of them, they didn't hold any animosity against me. Some of my American blunders were offensive to them, but instead of becoming angry with me, they used these incidents as teachable moments. They respected me enough to invest their time and energy into communicating with me, and I am still reaping the benefits of that gift today.

While in Zimbabwe I fell in love with the people. My calling in missions started to take shape as I spent the summer reporting to qualified, committed Christian leaders there and recognized that they lacked the resources needed for ministering to their people. When I returned to the States, I knew my role was to provide tools for the nationals to continue ministering effectively. What I didn't know yet was what tools I could provide.

As this idea continued germinating, it required me to deal with the wounds and lingering emotional pain from junior high. I clung to the biblical promise, "You will know the truth, and the truth will set you free."[25] Scripture was an essential ingredient in the healing process, but two years after returning from Zimbabwe, I realized I needed additional help with my emotional battle. So I sought professional counseling from Dr. David McKay.

Now as my three-hour wrestling match with God continued, I was reminded of an event from three years earlier, in 2000, when I had considered selling my bicycle. I had wondered if selling my bicycle would eliminate the constant, painful reminder of my love for cycling, which CFS had stolen from me. I mentioned it to my friend Jen. She interrupted me and stated adamantly, "You cannot sell your bicycle. Selling your bicycle means you're giving up hope!" Her words jolted me. Jen was right. I kept the bike.

During prayer I sensed God was asking me to give away $1,200, the cost of my bike, as an extension of giving myself away to God. I finally got it. Now there were just two things that needed to happen before I could fall asleep: I needed to write a letter, and I needed to write a check. By 11:30 p.m. the wrestling match had ended. God had won . . . but so had I.

The first thing the next morning I stopped by the Lutembekas'. John answered the door and invited me in. After I handed him the envelope, he proceeded to read the letter out loud.

The Lord gave me a big call tonight. He challenged me to partner with you in Tanzania by giving $1,200 to buy bikes and spare parts. Due to my health, I can't do much riding now, but cycling has taught me to live for Jesus. On our cross-country trips, Wandering Wheels' mission was threefold: To grow up in God, to give God away, and to ride coast-to-coast.

As I have given myself away to God over the years, now I want to take this opportunity to "give God away" in Tanzania by riding on faith. The Lord is asking me to give when it would be easier to say, "I will need this money." Yet I know that to truly give God away to others requires faith.

Since 1983, when I went to Zimbabwe, I have prayed that the Lord would let me partner in ministry with the African people by providing some kind of tool. Will you ask the bike recipients to pray for the growth of this idea and to pray for me? I pray that God will be given away to many, and that those receiving Jesus would grow up in God and repeat the cycle.

After reading the letter, John said, "Do you know how many people will be reached for Christ because you gave?" Expressing their gratitude, John read from Philippians 4:10-20: "I rejoiced greatly in the Lord. . . . You sent me aid. . . . Not that I am looking for a gift, but I am looking for what may be credited to your account. . . . And my God will meet all your needs according to his glorious riches in Christ Jesus."[26] Then Carolyn prayed for me. Of all the things she said, one line especially stood out to me: "You asked the widow at Zarephath to give to Your work before You gave her food to feed her son."

I went home, basking in a sense of *mission accomplished*. When I retrieved my mail, the first envelope I opened contained a $200 check with a note: "To cover medical bills." Next, I listened to my answering machine. "Alice, this is Pastor Love [the overseer of the benevolence fund]. I am calling to check up on how you are doing. How is your health? Your job? Please give me a call."

A deaconess from church had informed him of the difficulties I had been facing. When I returned the call, Pastor Love asked how the church could help. I told him the only bill I currently had was my six-month car insurance premium. The church covered it for me. By the end of the week, the $1,200 and my next six months of car insurance had been covered without anyone knowing the amount I'd given. Sure enough, God was providing for me, just as he had for the woman at Zarephath.

I could only imagine the financial management lectures I would have gotten if I'd told my friends and family how much I gave to buy bikes in Tanzania. However, the act of obedience was fundamental to the new dream God was forming in my heart: to give away a hundred bicycles during my lifetime. It was beyond my resources, but I refused to let CFS steal another dream from me!

On New Year's Day 2004, while I was having devotions, Luke 1:45 resonated in my heart. I made it my verse for 2004. "You are blessed because you believed that the Lord would do what he said."[27] I wrote:

> *Living God, I will depend on You this year to bring life to my bicycle work. Send the wind of life through the villages of Tanzania. Also, send the pastors forth on bicycles in the power of the Holy Spirit.*
>
> *Lord God Almighty, I surrender my life to You. I trust You to provide for my every need. "Not by might, nor by power, but by my spirit, saith the LORD of hosts."[28] I long to obediently follow Your direction.*

I was amazed at all the things God was doing, even though I was still bogged down in my CFS reality. In February 2004, I heard that Social Security disability insurance had reconsidered my case. I began what would turn out to be a yearlong, stress-filled wait for a hearing date to find out if I was eligible for benefits. Thankfully, my health grew somewhat stronger throughout the year. A quote I read by Anais Nin struck a chord in my heart: "Living never wore one out so much as the effort not to live."[29] So I was living life, hoping God was healing me and hoping my disability nightmare would end.

About ten months after buying the bikes for Tanzania, I sensed I was to give bikes away again. This time it happened at a church meeting in October 2004. While a missionary to Nigeria closed his presentation with prayer, I felt moved to give. After praying about it, I darted straight toward him and asked if bicycles would help his ministry. He said yes and asked, "Could I use half of your money to buy and distribute five hand-pedaled wheelchairs that are built locally in Jos, Nigeria?"

The missionary went on to explain that those with polio or with other lower extremity disabilities use wooden blocks for hand shoes, dragging their legs behind them. A hand-pedaled wheelchair (often referred to as a trike), would offer them independence and dignity. Having experienced physical limitations myself, I longed to make life a little easier for others with disabilities. My eyes were starting to open to the huge need that was out there.

In addition to the trikes, the missionary also bought five basic single-speed bikes for seminary students at Oyi River Seminary in Egbe, Nigeria. The students needed bicycles for traveling to their internships, which were church plants in rural and bush areas. The same month I gave $1,200, I made $1,200 working at my cousin's dental office. It was the first month in more than four years that my health permitted me to work that many hours.

Before the month was over, I received pictures of the trike recipients. It was startling to see a picture of a schoolteacher dressed in a three-piece suit, walking with his hand blocks and dragging his legs behind him. It melted my heart to see the smile and the hope on each recipient's face. An extra blessing was knowing these projects were supporting the national economy.

Before I knew it, my bicycle dream was getting bigger than bicycles!

The Wheels Start Turning

By the end of October I received pictures of the trikes I had just bought through the missionaries in Jos, Nigeria. The first show-and-tell was with my small group Bible Study, which had been meeting weekly for the past five years at the Walkers' home.

Bob Walker, then ninety-two, had been my friend and mentor for years. He encouraged me on a regular basis that despite my disability, "God still has a plan for your life, Alice." Over the years Bob also reminded me, "Barbara and I pray daily for you." Now God was using Bob to help me further embrace His call.

When Bob saw the pictures of the trikes, he said, "You must form an organization and incorporate the ideas God has given you. This vision is larger than your personal goal of giving away a hundred bicycles."

What had Bob just said? Hadn't I just stated that my personal dream was to give away a hundred bikes? Where had his wild idea come from? I didn't think I'd ever had aspirations of becoming an executive director of an organization. Or had I?

After our small group meeting, I shared our conversation with my brother. As Dan laughed and started getting excited about the idea, excuses barreled through my head. I had an answer for why it wasn't the right time, why I wasn't the right person, and why it wasn't the right idea. I felt out of control, without answers, unable to articulate the next step. I was in way over my head, without a clue about how such lofty talk could ever become a reality.

Besides, what business did I, a disabled person, have thinking I could start an organization? When I shared my well-formed rebuttal, Dan said, "Do you know who you are talking to? Alice, you were born to lead an organization." He must have been a pacesetter, because after talking to him, I couldn't find anyone to confirm my well-rehearsed excuses.

For me, beginning a bicycle ministry meant heading down an unknown road. Before I could embark on that path, I needed to do some serious soul searching. Days later, on October 31, I wrote the following prayer entry:

Beginning today I make a pact with You, Lord, to pray for this bicycle ministry idea daily for six months. If it is part of Your plan, may Your Holy Spirit provide divine direction down the road this is to take. You know all the things we need—a name, a mission statement, a board of directors, a logo, and funding.

During prayer, some heart-paralyzing fears and doubts surfaced. I wasn't sure I wanted to awaken, let alone face, these issues that felt like giants to me. As in the Bible account of David and Goliath, my fear-filled Goliaths seemed ten feet tall too. But if I just chose to leave them sleeping, in essence I was making the decision to remain complacent and settle for a life of mediocrity. I wasn't willing to let that happen. My fears were not going to dictate my future and steal such a great adventure from me.

I was glad Bob, Dan, and other people close to me wouldn't allow me to let these giants hold me captive. Every time I saw Bob he would ask how things were going with the ministry and suggest the next steps needed to bring it to fruition.

One week at Bible study I asked myself, *How will I come up with a name?* Next thing I knew, the word *His* came to mind. Bob, who was sitting next to me, was a word specialist. He had chosen *His* for InterVarsity's first campus ministry magazine. I was fascinated with the title and its versatility, especially as I considered the possibility of working in countries where the name of Jesus is hated. *His* would create curiosity and initiate a conversation about Jesus when people asked, "What does 'His' stand for?"

The bike ministry idea was His vision, which came through the leading of His people, to do His work, in His way. Thus, it made sense to call the organization His Wheels, leaving it broad enough to incorporate vehicles with two, three, or possibly four-wheels in the future.

My next step was to do an Internet search of the name *His Wheels*. My heart sank when I found that a Christian motorcycle organization had a chapter in Texas called His Wheels. It was back to the name game. Since my passion was getting bicycles to Africa, I considered His Wheels Africa.

However, when I shared the idea with the missionary from Nigeria, he said, "You can't limit this ministry to Africa, because I believe God has bigger plans than just Africa. Why not make it His Wheels International?" I liked the name, but imagining an international ministry felt like another ten-foot giant. However, since I knew it wasn't an option to allow fear to become a barricade, I proceeded, and the name was born.

Before making the name official, I wrote a letter to the Texas motorcycle chapter and asked permission to use His Wheels International (HWI). They inquired about our mission, offered to promote it, and thanked me for asking.

During prayer one night in November, three weeks after selecting the name, a picture came to me for the logo. I drew out the idea of three skinny tire wheels, each representing a member of the Trinity, enclosed by a fourth, heavier wheel that enveloped the three inner wheels. A friend from Denmark later said, "The outer wheel makes me think of the world."

The next Sunday I shared the logo with my Sunday school class. Afterward one member connected me with someone else from our church who owned a marketing business. He offered to turn my hand-drawn picture into a professional logo, gratis. I realized that none of these resources or ideas were chance happenings. They were divinely orchestrated, and my job was to continue moving forward.

With each new turn on this bike journey, I was learning new things about God, ministry, and myself. One important rule on God's road is that when things look hopeless, He is waiting to answer our prayers and reveal His master plan. Indeed, I was learning that He was big enough to use my disability and limitations for His glory. My part was being obedient to His plan. Of course, God was capable of taking care of all the other logistics.

After twelve years of battling CFS, sidelined from life,

I was about to see how critical those years of preparation were for the leadership position awaiting me. In His creativity, the sovereign God had a plan to give me the desires of my heart,[30] highlighting them with threads of my passions and experiences. I was both excited and terrified about embarking on the road ahead.

As I was preparing for this new adventure, I could see how my singleness was, in many ways, a gift. Being single gave me the freedom to focus my undivided attention, energy, and strength on listening to Christ and living for Christ. I could risk and invest all my resources in responding to Christ's call. The fact that I was single didn't mean I was alone. The Lord, along with my support network, was encouraging me to ride on in faith.

Seven years earlier, my pastor had challenged me to move to DuPage County, where I both worked and attended church. This initially seemed like a surprising call, since I had always sensed that my ministry would somehow include serving the poor. Having only worked with the poor in big cities in the past, I assumed He wanted me to stay in Chicago. But God continued to use different people and circumstances to confirm the pastor's words, so I began the moving process.

The day of the move, while driving to my new apartment, I sensed God say, "You will serve the poor in a bigger way from DuPage County than you would have in Chicago." I couldn't imagine how, given that the county's median household income at the time was more than $25,000 higher than the national average and only 4 percent of the population lived below the poverty line.[31] But the scales were soon going to fall from my eyes.

In January 2005 I set up four meetings to determine the viability of HWI as an organization. On January 12, God gave me an affirmation, via a follow-up letter from the Lutembekas.

> *Dear Alice,*
>
> *The bikes have served the cause of Christ in Tanzania. The evangelists in Dar Es Salaam and the Coast Region were enabled to reach more villages with the gospel of Christ. . . . One bike was given to the evangelist in Zanzibar. Other bikes were sent to Tanga, Muleba, and Karagwe. The report we have is that the evangelists praise the Lord for hearing their prayer for the bikes. They are reaching more people than before.*

On the same day I received the letter from the Lutembekas, I also went to my Social Security disability insurance hearing, having waited over a year for the hearing date. As the lawyer prepped me for the hearing, he said, "I don't think we have a chance at winning any part of today's case, but we will try. Your work record shows that even with CFS, you have lived at a high functioning level. That won't bode well for SSDI."

As my tears fell, my friend and former nursing instructor comforted me. She reminded me that God was in charge. Teary-eyed and trembling, I entered the courtroom.

After being sworn in, I took a seat.

"Do you still have fainting spells, or was this a one-time occurrence?" the medical expert asked.

"I have them regularly. Often, when I stand up from a seated position, my heart beats so hard it feels as though it will beat out of my chest. I have come close to passing out on numerous occasions."

The medical examiner thanked me, turned to the judge, and gave a medical diagnosis code. Subsequently, he gave a second diagnosis code, in case SSDI rejected the first one.

The judge then said, "Based upon the testimony of the medical expert, the administrative law judge finds that the claimant has been under a disability. She is therefore entitled to disability insurance benefits."

After the closing comments, we left the courtroom. The lawyer was stunned. The medical examiner knew it and said to him, "You didn't think you had a chance with this case, did you?"

I received both financial and medical components of SSDI, with back pay for the past two years. God had gone before me into the courtroom.

Even though I had increased my workload to part time three months earlier, I realized my health could no longer sustain that amount of work. God already knew my health limitations. The medical component of SSDI went into effect the day my employment health insurance benefits expired. God's timing, again, was perfect. My monthly SSDI check was fixed at $1,103. Once again, I was glad I had obeyed God in 1999 and paid off my home. Also, since my SSDI checks were retroactive and I had not incurred any debt during that time, I was able to tithe $2,800 of my check to start HWI.

For our initial four planning meetings, the HWI team

met every other week between February and March of 2005. The planning team included Harvey Lyon, whom I rode through Israel with seventeen years earlier. Harv had biked through twenty-eight countries by then, and during his seventy-eight years of life, he had gained a wide array of knowledge, covering an expansive list of subjects.

Although Harv was an atheist, he respected my religious convictions. I had convinced myself that he would only join us for the planning meetings. A few years later I learned that Harv is a business consultant, and his website is RentMyHead.com. I didn't know all that about Harv then, but I knew HWI needed his head.

Another person who joined us just to encourage me during the first four meetings was Louise Troup, then eighty-five. Louise was my pediatric nursing school instructor back in 1983 and has remained a friend and "bouncer" for over twenty years. We both attended the same Bible study group. Having lived her life of singleness to the fullest, Louise has always had time to offer me a listening ear. As a great communicator, she knows when to listen and when to share her experiences through the "retrospectoscope." Now she aligned with Bob, affirming that I needed to pursue HWI.

Back in 1941, as a Wheaton College student, Louise and her best friend Carol Erickson Smith had founded Pioneer Girls and Camp Cherith. The ministry's slogan was, "Christ in every phase of a girl's life."[32] Now, seventy years later, the name has been changed to Pioneer Clubs, but the International ministry is still vibrant.

Within a year of starting Pioneer Girls, Louise left to get her master's degree in nursing. Then it was off to South Africa as a missionary, where she began a school of nursing for Zulu and Swazi girls. The pennies, nickels, and dimes that Pioneer Girls around the country gave as their weekly club offerings supported her for seven years while she was on the mission field.

In 1984, at my nursing school graduation, my brother, Dan, met Louise and said to me, "I can see who you are modeling your life after." Dan nailed it. He saw the maverick twinkle in her eye, and was fascinated by the warmth that exuded from her presence and the enthusiasm with which she lived life. A question that burned in Louise's consciousness as a teen is now what she passes on to everyone she meets. "Can you be a Christian and still have fun? And God answered 'yes.'"[33]

Also, Bob, then ninety-two, attended our first meeting. What a historic event it was since, sixty-four years earlier, one of the first organizations Bob helped start was Pioneer Girls. His Wheels was the other bookend of Bob's flourishing legacy of organizations he helped start. He told me the same things he had told Louise back then. "You need a brochure with a succinct message, so others can catch the vision."

Upon Bob's death in 2008 at the age of ninety-five, through an obituary article, I learned he was "a pioneer in Christian periodical publishing and the last surviving founder of the Evangelical Press Association."[34] Bob's progressive loss of memory left him housebound soon after our first meeting, but he still encouraged me up until his death.

Bob also suggested I invite Tom Richards, another long term Bible study member, to join us. "He would be a good person for you to have on your board," he said. Then sixty, Tom was an avid cyclist. He had worked as a distribution center manager for years, but was now driving a school bus, caught in the out-sourcing craze of that era. Tom's strong

Christian faith, shepherding heart, and vast experience in Christian ministry made him an asset for our planning meetings.

Then Tom invited Greg Anderson, owner of Spin Doctor Cyclewerks and the shop owner from whom he bought his bike. Greg saw his store as an extension of his ministry, shining Christ's light into the community while providing trustworthy and outstanding service. Six years prior, Greg had traded in his hectic life working at the Chicago Mercantile Exchange, to pursue his passion. A year earlier, when God blessed the shop in profits, he gave five bikes away to missions in Haiti. His suggestion was, "Whatever you do, begin small."

Another person I invited was Cheryl Nguyen, a friend who was working full-time in a fund raising position. She was happy to join us for the first meeting but said, "The person you really need is Jeff Messer." So she invited Jeff, and he joined our planning meetings and also became a founding board member. Jeff, a thirty-three-year-old husband and father, couldn't find enough free time for cycling.

Jeff read every issue of Bicycling Magazine. He held memberships with the Chicagoland Bicycle Federation (now Active Transportation Alliance), League of Illinois Bicyclists, and League of American Bicyclists. His position as a product development engineer paid the bills, but cycling and joining our team topped off his cycling tank.

Another invitation went out to Tim Morgan, who had been deputy managing editor at Christianity Today International (CTI) for twelve years. CTI is a not-for-profit ministry, founded by Billy Graham in 1956.[35]

Their mission is "Creating Christian content that changes the people who change the world."[36] Tim's work had taken him on assignment around the world by the time I met him, months earlier, while auditing a journalism class he taught. I knew we'd benefit from his global input and expertise.

Tim felt his strengths would best be utilized as a consultant. He helped us formulate a media press release, and provided suggestions of where to send it. He also helped us brand HWI, providing brochure consultation and sharing ministry contacts with us.

I also invited Dan Easley, one of the benevolence committee members I had served with. Dan was happy to offer input during the initial meetings, but didn't have the time to commit to serving on the board. Dan was a computer guy who had business knowledge. He had served in a variety of church leadership positions, and had a heart for missions and those in need. Common sense made it a delight to work with him. Also in attendance for our first meeting was Antonio, a Latin American immigrant who lived in Chicago and worked as a graphic designer. He also built websites. I had met him only weeks earlier as we ministered together at a prison.

During our first meeting we discussed the need for a brochure, a website, and making sure we stewarded the finances well and handled them with the utmost integrity. At that meeting we also decided that HWI would not incur any debt in order to run the ministry. We also made it a priority to find an accountant to manage our finances, and an outside tax accountant to prepare our taxes.

Another suggestion that emerged from the initial meeting was for me to contact Bob (Coach) Davenport, founder of Wandering Wheels. When we talked, he told me how Wandering Wheels had bought bikes in Mexico for pastors one year. When Wandering Wheels returned the next year, they found the bikes and parts had been sold. Coach had become discouraged by that experience, and stopped doing it. The lessons Coach learned provided discussion material for our second meeting. We brainstormed possible checks and balances we could implement to decrease the chance of this happening with the bikes we would give away.

Also by the second meeting, I had come up with our theme verse, "Have I not commanded you? Be strong and courageous. Do not be frightened, and do not be dismayed, for the LORD your God is with you wherever you go."[37] In addition, we narrowed our initial focus to Africa.

By the second meeting I had contacted Rise International, a ministry located in Northfield, Illinois, thirty-two miles from Wheaton. Rise's mission is rebuilding lives and communities (in Angola, Africa) through education. They build schools, train teachers, foster partnerships, and lead teams on a Pilgrimage of Service to Angola.[38] Lynn Cole, the executive director, told me they were filling a container full of school supplies in the Northwest Suburbs, and had room for four bikes. In addition, Lynn inquired about getting a couple pumps, basic tool kits, additional tires, tubes, a patch kit, and locks.

Next question was, where would we get the bikes? Greg had two in his shop that were perfect for sending to Africa. He also offered to help us on an ongoing basis to collect used bikes, answer questions, and buy parts for HWI at cost. Before long we'd gotten three more bikes—one that was found in the trash, one that was donated by a local bike shop, and my dad's single-speed Schwinn that was hanging in my garage. By the third meeting we had five bikes, and Bob Walker donated $100, which was enough to cover the other bicycle items Rise had requested.

The next task was to repair four bikes. As Tom and I did that in my backyard, I paused to remember a stress-filled teen scene that would make us cackle for years to come.

After my first coast-to-coast trip, I ventured out to try and fix my bicycle as I had watched the Wandering Wheels mechanics do with ease. I enjoyed working on my bicycle, and had mechanical aptitude. But on one occasion, before I began working, my dad, who was not mechanically inclined, said, "Just take it to Jake's Bike Shop. I will pay to have it fixed."

I shot back in a petulant tone, "Will you pay for my bike to get fixed for the rest of my life?"

Dad shouted, "No!" Thus, I began to fix my bike.

After about an hour I hit an impasse, now having a pile of loose pieces and no clue how to reassemble them. But the worst was yet to come, the three-mile car ride with dad driving me to Jake's. You could have heard a pin drop, and the tension between us created an impenetrable barrier. What a relief when we pulled up to the store and my dad put the car in park.

I jumped out, leaving the ear splitting silence behind. I moved towards the trunk, untied the rope holding the hood down, and took my bike frame out. I proceeded to hang the frame over my right shoulder. I removed the rear wheel and tucked it under my left arm. With my hands free, or so I thought, I tried to balance the loose pieces. Of course, it never occurred to me to put the parts in a little bag. So, while attempting to walk and then open the store door, I left a trail of nuts and bolts behind.

One of the employees met me at the door. As I straightened up from bending over to pick up the loose parts from the ground, I caught him shaking his head back and forth. The expression on his face said it all. *Why are you trying to carry all that at once?*

Once inside I spotted Jake, a tall, wrinkled man. There was grease in the creases of his fingers that was older than I was. He took my bike to the back of the store, while I trailed along. As he put it up in a stand I thought, *Wow I'd like one of those someday.*

The shop smelled of bicycle lubricant, and new rubber tires. That scent was forever imprinted on my brain. I didn't know what to look at first. I heard the *pssss* sound of air being pumped into tires while the compressor vibrated. Those were lullaby sounds for a bicycle lover like me. My head was spinning. *Wouldn't it be fun to have a bike shop one day?* I pondered, *Complete with a set of those nifty blue plastic handled bicycle tools with white letters.*

By now my eyes were focused on Jake, and I was mesmerized by watching him put the pieces of my bike back together. *He could have done that in his sleep!* I thought. I dreamed of one day being able to pop a bike in the stand, fix it in record time like Jake, and then bask in the thrill of such an accomplishment.

After getting my fix of the bike shop, it was a relief to walk out with my bike fixed, no longer afraid that maybe somehow I had ruined it. Jake didn't know it, but he had sure created a more peaceful ambiance for our car ride home. I don't think my dad knew then that his ability to say no would one day become an ever-growing asset to his retirement savings plan.

In May 2005, when I drove out to Rise's container site with the bikes and requested items to sail for Angola, Africa, I experienced the sweet taste of victory. It was similar, yet different, to the one I had dreamed of as a teen, back at Jake's Bike Shop.

A further perk was being a participant in the larger work God was doing. I was astounded by His miraculous provision of all the resources we needed, finances, people, and bikes. Before we had even officially formed as an organization in May, I had several bikes in my garage. So when Louise, my mentor, gave us our second $100 check, we used the money for lumber. It was to reinforce the ceiling joists in my small garage, making it possible to hang fourteen bikes while still leaving room for my car. However, in no time bikes were spilling out of my garage.

On the administrative side, we finished our four initial meetings, and now I was trying to navigate the State incorporation filings. The next step was forming the board. Since Tom and Jeff had already agreed to join the board, I would make the third board member, fulfilling the legal requirements. Given that Harvey didn't share the organization's religious stance, I hadn't considered inviting him onto the board.

However, as I sought counsel from each of the planning committee members, they were adamant about inviting Harvey to join the board. The response surprised me, but I was not opposed, so I invited Harv onto the board. He was delighted, and went on to tell me he had served on several boards, but HWI provided him with a first, the opportunity to serve on a Christian board. By our first official board meeting, Harv said, "Do you know how much razzing I get when I tell my friends I'm going to Wheaton for a Christian board meeting?"

I threw that one right back at him. "Do you have any idea how much explaining I must do when I tell my Christian friends that I have a Jewish atheist on HWI's board?" When I've told people, eyes bulge, jaws drop, and out come *ahhh* sounds. Some have disagreed with our decision to invite Harv onto the board. But I've never had anyone disagree with our decision after they meet Harv. He has helped open our eyes up to many things, not least of which is the cryptic, insular, foreign language Christians speak.

It was obvious from the very beginning that Harv made sure we kept true to our Christian mission, and didn't veer off into just another humanitarian organization. In one press release, I didn't put in the word Christian. He questioned me as to why I left it out. I said, "Harv, if I put the word Christian on the first line, some won't take the next step and explore who we are."

He said, "I never thought about that, but you are right!"

Whether HWI or Harv has benefited most from his part as a founding board member, depends on who you ask.

Since this is my memoir I will tell you, HWI and I have benefited most.

Not only was I a rookie, but I also didn't have any idea what was needed to begin HWI. At several junctures I couldn't comprehend why He had chosen me as the executive director with all my limitations. I found myself saying, "Lord, you know I'm not capable!" Yet the truth of scripture returned. This time in the book of Jeremiah through the words, "Before you were born I consecrated you."[39]

Apprehension loomed in my heart. I still couldn't predict if I could get out of bed from day to day, not to mention working or doing anything else on a regular basis. Whatever the HWI plan was going to look like, it had to take into account my inability to live an ordinary life. One thing I knew was that I could network, and find people who had bikes to get rid of, even if I could only do it piece-by-piece, day-by-day, week-by-week, as my health allowed. At the core of my being, I knew I could always serve the Lord somehow, within the boundaries of my limitation.

Feelings of doubt were mixed with excitement now, because I had always wanted to be involved in full-time Christian service. However, the magnitude of this new assignment was humbling. Yet with the Lord's help and the encouragement of my support team, I embraced my new role as the executive director of HWI and begin organizing our new "cycling team."

I was beginning to see that my CFS limitations were a team-building asset, allowing others to participate as our dreams were unfolding. For example, Harvey's words encouraged me one day. He said,

Alice, you have responded like Job, "Though He slay me, yet will I trust in Him." You didn't say, "Who needs You, God, if this is what You have done to me?" Through it, you found out how steadfast your faith was as you learned to work within the limits of CFS. The combination of your vision and your limitations has given others the opportunity to say, "Here is a woman who doesn't know if she can get out of bed tomorrow, but knows she can do God's work, so let's help."

I also came to realize I couldn't create something bigger than myself. My limitations were unpredictable, and it was important for me as a leader to know my strengths and weaknesses. As a result, it made me depend on delegating, and relying on other people, which, for a perfectionist like me, was a terrifying thought. My number-one priority in ministry was to care for and maintain my body, His temple. Yet, regardless of the health consequences I experienced from taking on added responsibilities, I still managed to get up and come back. In my weakness, I experienced the Lord's faithfulness.

Following God's leading forward was much more liberating than following the rules of the world. A crucial management lesson I learned was not trying to do more than I could, but doing everything I could. This meant HWI needed other specialists on our team, to help us function effectively while moving forward. Part of the process was finding out what others could do, and then letting them do it on the road to reaching their ultimate ministry potential.

Harv helped us as a board by identifying the challenges we had to work through. He said to me,

The original board's job is to help you to flesh out your vision within your disability limits, with the added challenge of beginning without any financial base. We have to figure out how we can help you, the executive director, whose dependability is unpredictable. In so doing, we have to consider what steps we can take so that something happens every day, even if you can't do something every day. We need to create a next step, something that is there and ongoing every day so we have the energy to keep HWI moving forward, rather than falling on our faces and having to start from the beginning again. In essence, we are beginning to create a virtual corporation, farming everything out to others.

On May 19, 2005, as I dropped the state-mandated paperwork in the mail for our incorporation status, I prayed for God's blessing and direction. Now the HWI team and I would seek to fulfill the mission of mobilizing God's work worldwide by providing bicycles and bicycle expertise to nationals, both in the United States and throughout the world.

Our vision included collecting, refurbishing, and redistributing used bicycles. The mission was fueled by our passion for bicycles, God's Word, and our neighbors around the world. We had no idea then how many neighbors throughout the world we were setting out to meet. But I was holding on tight to God, because if this bicycle trip was like any of the other ones I'd taken, there was no telling where the road would lead.

Forming Our Team

One day in April 2005, I stopped by St. Andrew Church in West Chicago at the suggestion of Louise, my mentor, to observe their Hispanic outreach ministry. Within an hour of our unannounced visit, Louise had pulled together our first HWI event-planning meeting. Those in attendance were pastors and ministry leaders from their Anglo and Hispanic congregation. By the time I left that meeting, the pastors had invited us to have three summer events at their church to launch HWI.

So between May and August 2005, we had three bicycle rallies at St. Andrew Church, a perfect location in terms of visibility and exposure. Since one of our goals was to assist refugees, we decided to begin by helping those who were part of the Hispanic congregation. Other events included performing bicycle safety checks, showing a video on how to properly size and wear a helmet, and hosting a bicycle obstacle course. In addition, we had bike sales and bike collections. The media publicity and connections with potential new team members through "God-working" were beyond my expectations.

The first evidence of God at work came through an unexpected source—a conversation with my five-year-old nephew, Ben. "Aunt Alice, you aren't in charge of HWI."

That caught me by surprise. "Okay, who is?" I inquired.

"Well, see, God's in charge of HWI," Ben said, "and you and I, we are co-directors."

When I thought of who would be part of HWI's team, I hadn't considered that some of HWI's core members would include children. But Ben's wisdom was part of "God-working," helping me to see HWI through a bigger lens. Including Ben as my unofficial co-director gave Ben and me a ministry to serve in together. Ben's insights heightened my sensitivity to ways God might want to encompass children and their ideas into His work through His Wheels.

In addition to the program side of ministry, administratively, I had just filed His Wheels International as a not-for-profit entity in the state of Illinois. Next, I began the federal IRS 501 C-3 not-for-profit tax-exempt filing process. A month later I was ready to send off the twelve-page document. After having a lawyer review it, I hoped to mail the application the next day, along with the twenty-nine additional pages of information. Since I'd made a mistake on one of the pages, I needed to download the page from the Internet to make the quick corrections. That's when I discovered that in its place was a more comprehensive application, which had gone into effect months earlier. My heart sank.

But before panicking completely over the daunting

nightmare of starting over on another IRS application, I called Harv. "Help!" I said. "We're flunking out on our master's thesis."

Not exactly, but I sure had the nerve-wracking feelings that accompany finishing a project of such magnitude. Harv came over and helped me organize what still needed to be done. The form was so complicated that I couldn't even understand why they were asking such outlandish questions. But Harv understood them and was able to explain.

We were delayed in filing by only four days, and since June 8, 2005, was our first official HWI board meeting, the board members signed one of the needed documents. Our founding board consisted of Jeff Messer, Harvey Lyon, Tom Richards, and me.

I saw how forming the HWI team had many of the same components as beginning any of my Wandering Wheels trips. Prior to each trip I wondered who would become part of our team. Where would they come from? Why did they decide to spend their time in this way? Was it possible that one day our team, made up of a group of eclectic strangers, would become a cohesive team? What shared dreams, hopes, and memories would God use from the hours we clocked riding together?

The primary benefit of group riding over solo touring was the shared camaraderie, which would help us make it through each mile and ultimately fulfill the goal of crossing the finish line. A team complete with cooks, logistics coordinators, follow-up drivers, mechanics, and team leaders allowed the riders to invest precious energy into riding and completing the trip.

When one was weak another could lead, breaking the wind and making it easier for those who were having trouble making it through the day. I remember struggling one day just to make another pedal rotation. I was on flat ground, but I grasped for breath, my thighs burned, and I pushed against what seemed like a hundred pounds in the easiest gear. The fierce headwinds through the Iowa countryside left my spirits low and my energy in the negative zone. Then I heard chattering and laughter behind me. At the same time, I found my pedals turning as if I was floating through air. *What's going on?* I wondered. *Did a tailwind just come through and push me forward?* No. When I looked behind me, I saw Carla, my group leader, holding on to the white flagpole on my bike from which an orange safety flag flew. She was using her strength to assist me. Her boost provided a new burst of energy.

I felt the same boost from my new HWI team members on the everyday road. Harv's help filling out the IRS paperwork made it possible to mail it off the next day. Afterward, I went to the bank to open our account. The first deposit consisted of $170 from bicycle sales, $143 in donations, and a $250 loan from my personal account. By our July board meeting, our bank account had grown to $1,262, and HWI had paid me back the $250.

Since we were weak in finances, we put a strong

emphasis on creativity and networking. Knowing we needed a website, I thought of Eric, Jen's sixteen year-old-son. He had entered a website building contest the year before, drawing up an imaginary site. Knowing he hoped to study computer design in college and was planning to submit another website in five months for the same contest, I suggested he become our webmaster.

Eric was hesitant. He didn't have all the resources he needed, and he didn't want to start something he couldn't finish well. I knew he was interested, so I encouraged him to build the site and told him I'd find the resources he needed. I contacted a friend of mine who was a computer wiz. She was willing to consult with Eric and guide him, filling in the gaps of his technical knowledge.

It was a win-win-win situation. My friend got to share her knowledge with a sharp young man. HWI got a website. Eric got to see how his educational interests fit into ministry. We paid Eric $150 to build the site; then he went on to win a $500 college scholarship and a $100 cash reward two years in a row.

By the time of our second bicycle rally on July 17, 2005, word about HWI was spreading. I had been on Wheaton College's radio station and had a second radio interview scheduled with another station in a few weeks. Our event was advertised on Moody Radio and in a local paper, as well as on the St. Andrew marquis and in their church bulletin.

I invited an Ethiopian ministry leader who was studying at Wheaton College to speak at the rally about the value of a bicycle in Africa. "Think of all the places you drive your car," he said. "How would you like to walk all those places, especially in inclement weather? It becomes very discouraging. So much energy goes into just walking five or six hours to get to a village. That time could be better spent ministering to the people in the village." He explained how bicycles are a principal mode of transportation in many African countries, as in many countries around the world.

After the rally an acquaintance invited me to a meeting the next night. An Ethiopian government official from Washington DC was going to meet with a local group interested in helping those in Ethiopia. I didn't understand all of what was going to take place at the meeting, but it piqued my curiosity. Since the meeting was close to home, I decided to go, taking my HWI photo album with me. Before the meeting started, I showed the guest from Washington a picture of the hand-pedaled trike in Nigeria I provided funds for.

Imagine a wheelchair and a tricycle combined in one vehicle, where the rider uses his or her hands to pedal. The trikes we bought in Nigeria had two thin bicycle wheels in the back, as were common on the old one-speed bikes or racing bikes. The wheels were attached to outriggers on both sides, which allowed the wheels to spin. They had seats and floorboards made of flat metal. Out in front, where one would expect to find the handlebars on a foot pedaled tricycle, was the bottom bracket of a bicycle, where the gear and pedals attached. The gear system was connected to a chain going straight down to the rear gear hub, now located on a smaller front wheel. As a result, the pedaling, steering, and braking were all encompassed in the same hand-operated mechanism.

In Nigeria, many people who need a wheelchair cannot afford one. Instead, they use blocks of wood or sandals on their hands, like shoes, to protect them as they move along in a crawling type of motion. People with disabilities are often seen along the side of the road with their faces to the ground, navigating through dirt and sewage. A trike would allow a person to get up and out of the dirt—to look up and see the world from a brighter perspective. It would allow these individuals to travel further, while also providing a more dignified mode of mobility.

This mode of transportation enables them to gather firewood or water and participate in the life of the community. It provides a way for them to travel to school and gain an education. And for some, it is a way to carry cargo on their backs, creating a small rolling store for selling wares and allowing them to provide for the needs of their families. Trikes provide a way for disabled individuals, often viewed as outcasts, to become valuable members of their society.

I had accepted the invitation to attend this meeting just to observe, listen, and learn from the discussion about ways to help in Ethiopia. The primary ideas included building a medical and dental clinic, along with a fitness center. Yet the Ethiopian official couldn't stop mentioning the need for hand-pedaled trikes throughout Africa. He shared that there were many with lower-extremity disabilities resulting from birth defects or polio. Those injured by landmines would benefit from such transportation as well. Landmines were a grave legacy of the twentieth century, having killed and maimed millions worldwide.

After the meeting I couldn't get the idea of trikes out of my mind, and before long another dream was born. Now I wanted to take a welding class so I could build a trike. Even though my health condition made such a thing impossible, CFS couldn't steal my ability to dream.

The day after the meeting with the Ethiopian group, I awoke prepared for a midweek Sabbath rest. I turned off my phone and computer to eliminate distractions so I could give God my undivided attention for the day. My brain was spinning. I was in need of a day alone with God. Only three months after beginning HWI, I had more than sixty bikes in my backyard, and new things just kept happening.

While praying, I heard a knock, at my front door. Annoyed and short on patience, I went to answer. I wondered, *Who's there?* It was a stranger.

He pointed at the curb. "Are you throwing away those bicycle parts?"

Yes," I said, silently wondering, *Why are you bothering me to ask? What a stupid question!* He was referring to unusable scrap bicycle parts I had left out the night before in hopes that a metal scavenger would pick it up in the night.

"I see the bike rack on your car," the man went on. "You must be a cyclist."

By now I thought, *Would you just take the parts and leave me alone?* However, the Holy Spirit helped me to continue the conversation. I paused to regroup, and then I reached out my hand for official introductions.

As we walked to the backyard, I told Tom I was a cyclist and that three months earlier we had begun HWI. Tom, too, was a cyclist. He raced and had a couple of expensive bikes, including a racing bike that was worth more than $5,000.

By the time I met Tom, HWI had already distributed forty bicycles. Twenty-two were in African countries. The other eighteen had gone to immigrants, international students, Christian workers, missionaries, ex-offenders, and the homeless in our local community.

By now Tom was staring wide-eyed at me, a grin engulfing his face. While looking at our collection of bikes he said, "Oh, my goodness. I've never knocked on someone's door before taking bicycle trash at the curb, but for some reason I sensed I was supposed to knock. This could be a divine encounter."

Before long Tom shared how he had had a total hip replacement ten months earlier. As a result he was unable to continue his duties as a fireman, so he was forced into early retirement at age fifty-eight. Tom had a strong faith in God, but that difficult transition left him depressed and struggling to find purpose in life. He said, "Six years ago I went to bicycle mechanic school. Could I come over once a week and work on bicycles?"

By then we were both ecstatic. "Of course!" I blurted.

During our conversation I had told Tom there were eight bikes awaiting pick-up at a local bike shop. Tom said, "Jump into my van, and we can go pick them up right now." As we drove I thought, *Am I crazy? I've only known this guy twenty minutes! Why am I driving off to a bike shop with him?*

Tom began coming to my home two mornings a week. We set up shop in my driveway, and both of us worked on bikes. I had some tools by then, but Tom had a complete set of tools that he brought with him.

When I met Tom's wife, Carol, she said, "When Tom came home that Tuesday and told me he'd found a bicycle mission organization, I didn't believe him. I just rolled my eyes."

I asked her, "How has retirement been for you?"

With a grin on her face and a chuckle in her voice, she said, "Much better since Tom found HWI."

Tom's interruption that Tuesday was God's way of orchestrating His divine plan while also answering Tom's, Carol's, HWI's, and my prayers all at once.

The timing was perfect for HWI, because bikes kept coming in. News about HWI was getting around by word of mouth, through the airways, and in print. After fixing the bikes, I was anxious to get them to people who needed them. My home was located halfway between the World Relief DuPage refugee resettlement office and a local apartment complex where many of the refugee families lived. As the children passed by and saw us working, they began hanging around and wanting to help. As someone who likes to help, I just began giving these refugee children bikes without a system in place and without thinking about the ramifications of my actions.

The next day there was a knock at my door from one of the children I'd just given a bike to. The timing was terrible since I'd just gotten on the phone with my best friend, Jen. It was to be the type of call that would involve each of us pouring ourselves a cup of tea, wishing we were together in person, while hours slipped by like minutes. But having made eye contact with the child as he looked in my living room window, it was impossible to ignore the knock. I told Jen I'd call her back. When I answered the door, the boy said, "My cousin is here and needs a bike. Can you get him one now?" I went out and got him a bike right then, hoping I could resume my telephone conversation without further interruption.

Once back inside I reheated my cup of tea and called Jen back. About the time we were settling back into our conversation, there was another knock from another refugee. I couldn't ignore him because he, too, had made eye contact before knocking.

"The bike you gave me yesterday just needs some air in the tires," he said. "Can I borrow your pump?" I returned to the phone and told Jen to hold while I got the pump.

Just as I was ending my conversation, I got another knock. "The pump isn't working." By now I was downright agitated. When I went out to assess the problem, I found it had nothing to do with the pump. No, it was a flat tire. So I changed the flat. By then I was frazzled, tired, and miffed. The situation went from bad to worse over the next several days. Having given away more bikes, I was now getting a steady stream of visitors, beginning around 8 a.m. and going as late as 9 p.m., all wanting a bike or needing a major repair on a bike I had given away.

It took a couple of months for me to realize that my overzealousness and lack of planning were going to lead to my demise. I had to rethink what I was doing. What I came to realize was that giving things away for free breeds a fierce entitlement mentality. Since I had given these individuals the bikes, the bikes were still mine in their minds. So when something went wrong, it was my problem, which meant I was expected to fix the bikes right then and there.

I never wanted HWI to be Santa's alternative workshop, with me being the backup Santa Claus. But with HWI operating out of my home, that's exactly what was happening. I stopped giving bikes out haphazardly, but the knocks at my door continued for several months.

At our third bicycle rally in August 2005, Rick, a volunteer I'd met at the last rally, offered to help us set up for the event. Afterward he invited me to attend his fiftieth birthday party the next night. It wasn't a party I typically would have attended, but this time I did.

As I was leaving the party, God's next divine appointee had just arrived home, where the party was being held. A friend told me, "You need to talk to Kevin." However, he didn't appear interested in a conversation. His body language seemed to say he wanted to make a quick obligatory showing and then dart out again. I was reluctant to intrude on his time, but I introduced myself and showed Kevin the Nigerian trike pictures.

We stuck up an instant conversation. "I hope to take a welding class," I said, "to learn how to weld so I can build trikes."

Within minutes Kevin said, "I'm a mechanical engineer. Can I design, build, and pay for the trike prototyping?"

My heart skipped a beat. "Ahhhh, sure," I said. But sadly, as I left, the pessimism in my heart was quick to surface, and I thought, *This will never happen.*

However, within a week Kevin had designed our first prototype, a hand-pedaled low-rider trike. HWI was only five months old, and we were forming a new division—global trikes. Our plan was to help those in other countries with lower-extremity disabilities. We were off to a strong beginning down the research and development road.

Only three weeks after meeting Kevin, we were about to encounter an unexpected twist with a potentially devastating outcome for HWI. One day a businessman called and said, "I'd like to stop by tonight and talk with you about the trike." I had met him about a month earlier and we'd talked about ways he could help HWI get started.

I agreed to the meeting and immediately after hanging

up, I called Kevin. After explaining to him about the call, I said, "Please come for the meeting."

The businessman began by saying he'd like to help us get our trike into all the countries where he was working. Although his words were smooth, it wasn't long before I started getting a gut feeling that something wasn't quite right. He gave enough facts to sound convincing, but not enough for me to connect the dots. The only thing I gathered over our four-hour conversation was that he had made some type of communication bid to several government officials in foreign countries. Now he was just waiting for the final word of approval. He went on to explain how advantageous it would be if we partnered together. If he could offer the country a not-for-profit arm in the form of our trike, his bid would be more appealing. He guaranteed us that he would get our trikes into all those countries too.

During the conversation he also asked about our board and suggested his own list of board candidates. He advised me to call my board members the next day and inform them that these candidates would be up for election at our next board meeting, only four days away. By the time he left, I had agreed to work with him and had invited him to the board meeting.

But when I tried to sleep that night, I couldn't. I replayed the four-hour meeting over and over in my head. I couldn't prove anything, but it certainly seemed like he was manipulating me. He was trying to get me to deceive my board by presenting his list of names as if they were mine. The excitement of advancing our trike program around the world, before one trike had even been built, was enticing. But I didn't know what type of work he was doing, where he was doing it, or how he wanted to partner with us. It reminded me of the saying "If something sounds too good to be true, it probably is." The next day I called the businessman back and said, "Everything is off!"

At our board meeting we debriefed this scenario. I didn't know exactly what had just happened to me, but Harv did. He said, "One day we will be able to swim with sharks like that, but we aren't ready to do so now." His comment showed me how God had protected us from the first possible hijacking of HWI.

Six weeks after meeting Kevin, the low-rider trike was ready to ride. For the first time I asked Kevin, "Why were you so quick to volunteer to prototype a trike?"

Jokingly he said, "I felt sorry for you." Later he expanded on his answer. "As a manufacturing engineer, I had the knowledge to design something simple. You know, there are many things I could volunteer to do in church, but others could do them just as easily and probably better. This is a unique opportunity that encompasses my abilities and interests. Building the trike strongly parallels what I do for a living. I take something through the whole design process, including many steps after the project is complete. The average person does not have the knowledge, resources, or tools to navigate such a process on their own." It was clear that Kevin was just the man God had in mind for creating a trike division within HWI.

In November I contacted Dawn Clark, the disability ministry director at College Church in Wheaton, Illinois, to see if she knew anyone who could try the trike.

"I don't know if I can think of anyone," she said. "But I have another idea. My son, Jeremy, is in North Africa. He is looking for some type of disability ministry, and this may be a perfect project for him. Could you bring the trike by tomorrow?"

When we met with Dawn the next day, Kevin and I learned she was a physical therapist who had spent many years on the mission field in Papua, New Guinea. She went on to say, "We are leaving in less than a month to visit Jeremy and his family for Christmas. Could we take drawings and pictures of the trike to show him? He doesn't know how to weld, but he has always wanted to learn. Could you teach him how to build a trike and possibly send one back with him if he is interested?"

By the end of 2005 our trike design was heading to Africa, and the God-sized dream of HWI kept unfolding. On the bike side, we had received 242 bicycles from bike stores, bike collections, individual donors, and police pounds, and we had distributed seventy-five of them. Four went to Angola, Africa, and the other seventy-one were distributed to those in need nearby. An urban church partnered with us, and they distributed twenty-nine bicycles as Christmas presents to needy children through their local public school. One bike went to an ex-offender who was part of a Christian post-prison program. After spending eight years behind bars, he had only been on the outside for nine days. As he mounted his bike with a smile on his face, he said, "You put the first set of wheels under me in eight years. Thank you."

A God-sized tailwind was moving our team forward fast. It was exciting, but I felt out of control. In the midst of it all I faced a constant battle for balance between trying new things and not overdoing it. I was amazed at how God was using me, an unfit person with CFS, in such unexpected ways to magnify His glory. It was also staggering to see how God was building our team. In addition to allowing me to fulfill my dreams, the Lord was allowing our new team members to fulfill theirs, too. He was also allowing those serving in Africa to fulfill their ministry dreams.

God was using the talents and interests of several ordinary, weak, selfish people, just like me, to participate in His Kingdom work through His Wheels International.

In front of my house in Detroit
(age 3)

The bike my dad picked out
of the trash for me (1967)

Taking a break on my front porch
(age 5)

Right: My twin brother, Dan,
and me with our new bikes
(age 5)

Opening ceremony in Portland, Maine

Above: Mom and me (age 15) before my first coast-to-coast trip in 1977

Right: Carla Koontz (my group leader) and I prepared for the California desert sun.

Bottom:
Finishing 1977 coast-to-coast trip at Haystack Rock, Cannon Beach, Oregon (Photograph by Paul King)

Greeting a home health patient in 1992

Nursing school graduation, 1984
(Photograph by Ebert Photography)

Right: Bicycling
uphill from the Dead
Sea on the way to
Masada in Israel
(1988)

Bottom Right:
Carrying my bike up
Snake Path to Masada

The day I became a
homeowner (1998)

Alice, Dan, June (sister-in-law),
Mom, Ben, and Dad (2000)

"Jammin" with Ben in
my backyard (2002)

My mentor, Louise Troup,
and me (2010)

Harvey Lyon and me (2011)

Some of the bikes His Wheels bought in Tanzania

John and Carolyn Lutembeka and me (2003)

Below: My garage only months after His Wheels began

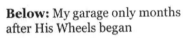

Above: First bicycle rally: Bob Walker, Dad, Alice, and Ben (2005)

Tom Egan, HWI's first mechanic

Prayer time with a church work group at the new His Wheels facilities (Photograph by Bill Koechling)

Left: Church work group helping us fix bikes on the second floor of our new headquarters (Photograph by Bill Koechling)

Above: Kevin Nikolich, our engineer, and Grant Burns, our bicycle coordinator, in our HWI workshop
(Photograph by Bill Koechling)

Right: Anika Lunde on the racing trike designed by Kevin Nikolich

Below: BJ Kettinger giving our first low-rider trike a test ride

Jeremy, who set up HWI's first trike manufacturing shop in North Africa

Left: This Ethiopian man walked through dirt and mud protecting his hands by flip-flops, as he searched for medical help for his disability

Right: Surgery was not an option, but Soddo Christian Hospital in Ethiopia was able to provide him with a His Wheels trike to assist with his transportation needs.

Crate full of 15 trike kits and one completed trike, bound for Ethiopia (2010)

Left: Maxene on his new trike in Haiti

Mile Markers

As 2006 began, I couldn't wait to meet with Dawn Clark to hear about her trip to North Africa and the reception our trike plans had received. When we met, she informed me that her son Jeremy was interested in partnering with HWI to explore a trike-building project. Our next step was for Kevin to send Jeremy a list of materials required for building the trikes. That way Jeremy could find out what was available in the local communities. Part of our goal for setting up small factories was to rely on supplies available in that country. We wanted to be careful not to create dependency by using supplies that had to be sent from the United States.

On the bike side of our ministry, our partnerships kept expanding. One connection was with the Cook County Forest Preserve in Illinois. They gave us fifty-nine bicycles in varied states of repair that had been abandoned or stolen and left on the county trails. We added those bikes to the forest of over two hundred bikes already in my backyard.

As the bikes piled up, we faced a frigid Illinois winter dilemma: it was no longer possible to fix the bikes outside. But there was no need to worry! God knew about that problem, too. So one Sunday in January, while I was talking with my mentor, Bob, at church, he asked, "How many bikes are in your basement now?"

I replied, "I don't have a basement. How many will fit in your basement?" I knew the first part of Bob's answer before he began, but I wasn't prepared for the second part.

Bob replied, "I don't have a basement, but this guy sitting next to me does!"

Without hesitation, Bob's ninety-two-year-old friend, Ken, piped in, "About one hundred could fit in our basement." I didn't know Ken, but I could see he was wearing hearing aids, so I wasn't sure he had heard the conversation or knew what he had just agreed to do. When he said, "our basement," I felt some relief, assuming his wife was probably the other party, and I hoped she would provide a reality check for this crazy idea. Still, unable to believe this scenario, I darted to the back of the church to find our board member Tom. There I explained what had just transpired and asked if he would follow up with Ken to make sure he understood what he'd just agreed to do.

After talking with Ken, Tom returned with his head bobbing up and down. He recounted his conversation to me. "Ken said, 'Yes, Alice is going to drop off one hundred bikes this week.'"

I said, "Yes, but what about his wife?" Tom informed me that Ken was recently widowed. I was stunned as I pondered this wild scenario—yet another one of God's provisions.

Prior to our bike drop-off day, I learned Ken had

white carpet in his basement. Concerned about this, I called him.

"Don't worry," he said. "I will roll it up."

But when we pulled up with the bikes, I had a few surprises awaiting me. I assumed there would be an entrance through the garage, directly down to the basement. Wrong! No one had mentioned to me that the only way to access the basement was through the beautiful front wooden door, over an ornate carpet in the hallway, then through the white-carpeted living room filled with antique furniture. The white carpet continued down the stairs, and at the bottom was a tight corner. By the time we finished unloading, the white walls in the stairwell were accented with marks from bicycle tire treads.

While carrying our first load through the house, I saw a picture of Ken's wife propped on a table in the vestibule. As I looked at her picture, embarrassment overcame me. I found myself talking to her: "I know, no woman in her right mind would be carrying bicycles through someone's whole house to get to the basement." When I admitted this to Ken, he assured me she would have been as excited as he was.

The basement was huge, having more square footage than my home and garage combined. It provided us with storage space and a place to repair the bikes. But even more important, our presence helped lift Ken's lonely spirits. His house was now filled with a flurry of activity and new life. When a neighbor asked him how he'd gotten involved, he said, "I don't know." I would have to say that Ken was guilty by association with Bob.

As HWI kept rolling along, I couldn't ditch the CFS stalker's antics. I couldn't evade the debilitating brain fog, bone-deep pain, and overwhelming fatigue. But one of the symptoms I finally got a better handle on was the wacky heart rate that made it impossible for me to stand for extended periods. For instance, I dreaded going shopping, knowing I might not make it through the checkout line without feeling faint. Another problem was standing in church to sing—something I had once taken for granted.

This condition, called postural orthostatic tachycardia syndrome (POTS), is commonly seen in CFS patients. It's marked by a consistent heart rate above one hundred beats per minute as a result of changing positions. It causes a jittery feeling that starts at the center of my being and works its way outward. The jumpy feeling caused by POTS has often been compared to an anxiety attack.

My doctor came up with a symptom management plan that included Kerlone, a medication to decrease my heart rate, and Midodrine, which decreased my feelings of faintness. I also got a special medical ice vest and neck wrap so I could go outside when the temperature was above seventy-six degrees. The new plan didn't resolve all the issues, but it sure helped.

As each new opportunity came for HWI, I faced a mixture of feelings. First, I experienced the adrenaline rush that accompanies the thrill of something new, but that was soon chased away by an adrenaline-ending crash. There I collided with the feeling of losing control, which was a challenge I didn't know how to navigate.

It reminded me of a memorable dialogue I'd had with my youth leader when I was sixteen.

"Alice, you never dream," she stated. "You must begin dreaming!"

My comeback was, "The problem is, all my dreams come true!"

By then I had already cycled cross-country twice. One of the things many teenage girls dream about is marriage, but I never did. I just assumed it was the norm in our culture, a stage of development that just happened. It never dawned on me that God would lead me in another direction—to embrace the gifts of singlehood.

In the same conversation my youth leader went on to suggest I read some fantasy by Christian authors like C. S. Lewis and Tolkien to get my imagination stirring. It was a good suggestion, but as a teen I kept my schedule so busy going, doing, working, and playing that I didn't make any time for being, reading, or dreaming. After all, for me, dreaming was scary.

Now, since CFS had struck, I was unable to go, do, work, or play as much. So I made time to read, pray, and dream. I was finding out that dreaming and watching my dreams unfold had many similarities to exploring the world by bike. Living them out stretched my resources, knowledge base, education, and life skills. In addition, it required utilizing the networking connections God had provided for me. Each new discovery was complete with new challenges. Thus, dreaming required taking risks and relying on God's leading.

While fully participating in the unfolding God-sized dream of HWI, nagging fears were never far behind. Would

CFS somehow destroy His Wheels like it had so many other things in my life? First, I had to acknowledge it as a fear. Then I had to turn it over to the Lord. With time, what I began to learn was that my condition, a potential hindrance to leadership, was an asset in disguise for building our volunteer team. My limitations caused me to rely more on teamwork, camaraderie, cooperation, ownership, and the skills of our volunteer work force, some of the same components I had also appreciated about bicycling with a group as opposed to solo riding.

To the outside world, my title was founder, but on the team, my most important role was as someone who prayed. Prayer was a divine networking tool that God used to create miraculous connections.

In Peter Drucker's research on volunteers, he references them as "unpaid professionals."[40] He goes on to say, "These knowledge workers demand responsibility—above all, for thinking through and setting their own performance goals. They expect to be consulted and to participate in making decisions that affect their work and the work of the organization as a whole. And they expect opportunities for advancement . . . a chance to take on more demanding assignments and more responsibility as their performance warrants."[41] So it was for our volunteers.

Another partnership we formed was with World Relief DuPage, the refugee resettlement organization located near the HWI headquarters. This was a better solution for providing an ongoing flow of bicycles for incoming refugees and immigrants in need of transportation, as opposed to randomly giving them away to those who stopped by my house at all hours of the day or evening.

An added benefit of our World Relief connection was

that we met Greg, an Eagle Scout candidate. We partnered with Greg and twenty young men from his local Boy Scout troop. He proposed that HWI could teach Scouts to repair bicycles, and in return, the Scouts could fulfill badge requirements by collecting and repairing bicycles. In the end, everyone benefited: Greg finished his Eagle Scout project, and twenty World Relief refugees received bikes.

Greg's dad stated, "It's hard to call this a service project. It makes me feel so good inside."

Through working with Greg and his team, I received the blessing of combining my loves for youth and for teaching. I was also learning that living out my dream was not only important for my life journey, but it was also part of the larger story God was writing.

It was obvious that HWI was bigger than any of the safe and predictable dreams I had conjured up. My past dreams that had been dashed and shattered encompassed only a small slice of my heart's desire, and God knew it. Over the years I would come to realize that His magnanimous plan for my life was to weave together all my gifts, skills, passions, talents, and lifetime experiences.

In early spring, while at a bike store, I met Jan, a bicycle mechanic. As we talked about HWI's story, I shared with her my dream and prayer to somehow get bikes to those devastated throughout New Orleans by Hurricane Katrina, which had hit in August of 2005. I told Jan I didn't have any contacts there. Her eyes got big, and she began to get fidgety while waiting for me to finish my sentence.

"My church, Naperville Presbyterian Church, has a partnership with a ministry in New Orleans," she said. "They send teams down regularly to do projects. One is going out late in 2006 and another in early 2007. I will be joining them."

Now the larger story God was writing through HWI would also include Jan and her bicycle dreams

HWI partnered with Jan and Naperville Presbyterian, and we began collecting bicycles. After two church workdays, with the help of thirty-five people of all ages, 150 bikes were fixed. In addition, a church member offered warehouse space to store the bikes. Then a couple who loved biking and had done mission projects in New Orleans drove a truckload of bikes there over Thanksgiving weekend. The Christian Community Development group was excited to be able to provide practical transportation as a ministry tool for assisting area residents.

Now as I reflected on all the things God was doing through HWI, I was reminded of a correlation between the random mile markers in life and those on the county, state, or interstate roads across America. Each mile marker only made sense in relationship to its place of origin. For me, they remained an unsolvable mystery. I think the only ones who really know the mile-marker systems across America are the "kings of the road"— truckers driving eighteen-wheelers. Even so, those markers helped me get a rough estimate of the distance we traveled on cross-country trips, since that was before the days of high-tech cycling odometers.

I was reminded of my longest one-day ride in 1977, from Harrison, Nebraska, to Casper, Wyoming. As we set out that day, I didn't know how all the mile markers would come together. Before we took off, I looked over my bike for trouble and checked the air pressure in my tires. Then I filled my water bottles, packed my daypack, and slathered myself with sunscreen. After that Coach gave a devotional, followed by general instructions for the day's ride.

He said, "Lunch is on Wandering Wheels today," which probably meant we wouldn't ride through a town big enough to find restaurants or grocery stores to buy our own lunch.

At the same time we mounted our bikes, our truck driver took off down the road to find a place for all sixty riders, plus staff, to spend the night. The different possibilities included churches, campsites, schools, VFW halls, under the stars, or a handful of other unique options.

As we filed out of Harrison, Nebraska, in our riding groups, the first green sign with white lettering we passed read:

Lost Springs, Wyoming
56 miles

That meant we'd reach Lost Springs five or six hours later. I anticipated the chance to find a restaurant or store to get some junk food—pop, candy bars, and chips—for a refueling feast.

The wide open road, filled with rolling hills I liked to refer to as "the Baby Swiss Alps," was blanketed by an expansive blue sky and only an occasional car. In the distance I could see herds of antelope prancing by and Burlington Northern Santa Fe Line trains rumbling past. The southwesterly wind through the endless miles of sagebrush prairie created extra resistance on each pedal stroke, and the basking sun above left me hot, sweaty, thirsty, tired, and hungry.

About two hours later we passed another sign that read:

Lost Springs
27 miles ahead

By then I couldn't wait for my junk food feast. What a disappointment to reach Lost Springs, Wyoming, and read:

Lost Springs
Population 1
Elevation 4,996[42]

To my chagrin, there wasn't any store in sight.

Around 4:00 p.m., we stopped for dinner at McDonald's and were relaxing. By then we had already ridden 102 miles. Since one hundred miles was our daily average, I assumed our night's lodging was only a couple of miles down the road. Wrong!

Coach hurried us along. "Let's move out. There's still another forty miles left to ride tonight."

My spirits sank. I was spent, having biked ten to twelve miles per hour for the last ten hours. This didn't make sense, since one of Coach's cardinal rules was to be off the road by dusk for safety reasons. However, that night my group ended up riding into Casper, Wyoming, by the headlights of our follow-up vehicle. We ended up riding fourteen hours that day for a grand total of 147 miles. And we'd made it by pedaling steadily one mile at a time.

Now in 2006, while continuing forward on our journey, I couldn't believe all the mile markers our growing HWI team was passing. I still didn't have any idea how God would pull all these different people together and allow us to accomplish our diverse dreams through HWI, but I believed God could see the bigger picture even when I couldn't.

Two more markers came when we partnered with a local Kiwanis club and a parochial school. Their one-day combined donation was one hundred bicycles. That was how many bikes I had set out to give away in my life.

Other mile markers included providing fifty bikes for a Christian group home in Chicago and 107 bikes for a rural church in Michigan that partnered with the local school district. Also, a missionary who received a bike through HWI and was on a two-year furlough began helping us weekly during our bike mechanic days.

He said, "I want to use my new bicycle mechanic skills as part of my ministry when we return to France."

In July 2006, when Jeremy returned to Wheaton, he and Kevin met. They first discussed the specifications needed for a trike that would go to North Africa. Then they customized the design for that part of the world. The result was our fourth prototype. One change from the original was to use wheelbarrow wheels, since they were available in that region of Africa. Also, since Jeremy would need to show the North African Department of Health the trike before beginning such a project, he suggested building a break-down model. If it fit into two boxes, it could go as extra luggage on an overseas flight.

Three months later Jeremy had learned how to weld and build a trike. By then he was ready to return to North

Africa, and he took the prototype with him. In addition, we sent some welding helmets to replace the piece of sunglasses material the welders there used for protection. We also sent small tools and three sets of hard-to-find parts. And God even intervened so that the airlines allowed it to fly free.

We'd tried to anticipate all the problems Jeremy might encounter in manufacturing the trike. One thing we never considered was that he'd have problems inflating the tubeless wheelbarrow tires. As it turned out, the pressure from the compressor wasn't strong enough.

Throughout the first two years, when people saw HWI, their first response was, "Wow, this is quite a ministry that you and your husband began!"

When I said, "No, I am not married," jaws dropped. As I accepted and embraced the gift of singlehood, I was discovering my full potential and providing a venue for others to uncover their dreams too. Singlehood gave me freedom to say yes, risking and investing all my energy and resources into my dreams. I could live out my passion while focusing my undivided attention on Christ's call for my life. It afforded me more time for prayer and service, unconstrained by the responsibilities a wife and mother must juggle. Through my life and the ministry of HWI, others had the chance to witness the spiritual mystery associated with singlehood. Some people told me they saw Jesus working in a new way as they witnessed how the Lord was my strength, my first love, and my fulfilling joy. HWI provided a platform for proclaiming the "reason for the hope that is in [me]"[43] and challenged others to accept the gifts God gave them, too. It also provided a venue for me to walk alongside others as they unwrapped their gifts and took the next steps on their own spiritual journeys.

As 2006 ended, HWI was featured on the radio, in the newspaper, in magazines, and at business clubs. *The Daily Herald* named HWI a top 2006 newsmaker in DuPage County. More than 143 different volunteers had clocked well over 1,538 volunteer hours. We started a junior mechanic bike repair program for children to help fix bicycles. One mother said, "This is not just a bicycle ministry but a great children's ministry, too."

We distributed 418 bicycles, 308 of which were distributed nationally. In addition, bikes were bought or sent to Nigeria, Tanzania, Kenya, and Angola. As our ministry increased in Africa, my love for the people there continued to grow. I gained a deeper understanding of Matthew 6:21. "Where your treasure is, there your heart will be also."[44]

HWI volunteers covered many team mile markers, which were both solo events and part of a larger story. I thought back to that long day in 1977, when I saw an empty pick-up truck go by. I had been tempted to yell out, "Truck driver, if you don't mind stopping, I'd like to throw my bike in the back of your pick-up and have you drive me past the remaining mile markers." I could now look back and see there was no shortcut for the cumulative mile markers I had to cover before becoming the executive director of HWI. The Lord Jesus Christ, the King of my road, had a system where all the pieces fit into the grand scheme of God's masterpiece.

Here I echo the words of Spurgeon: "When we come into the region where the Lord worketh, we come at once into contact with miracles, and walk in the midst of marvels. Then as we see grace upon grace, we have to cry, 'Oh world of wonders I can say no less.'"[45]

Celebrating Our Accomplishment

As 2006 ended, I expected to feel happy and energized by all the amazing things God was doing through HWI. Instead, I was struggling with mixed emotions.

Over Christmas my dad asked, "Alice how does it feel to be the founder and executive director of an international ministry?"

"Let's put this into perspective." I replied. "I'm a founder and executive director living on Social Security."

Later that day I wondered, *What provoked me to react with repulsion toward my dad's compliment?* The affirmations from friends over the past few months had left me feeling uncomfortable and confused. But Dad's comment was only the tip of the iceberg. I found myself wanting out, longing to run away and hide. But I didn't know what I was running from, or why.

What an irony—I wanted out, but my home was the legal address for HWI. The idea of abandoning my passion was as absurd as abandoning my home. The problem was, I knew I'd found my passion and that "he brought me out into a broad place; he rescued me, because he delighted in me."[46]

But I didn't know how to navigate the road ahead.

Indeed, by one standard I was a successful executive director. However, the words that blared the loudest in my head were those of the Social Security lawyer from my first visit in 2003. "By the time you've come to see me and apply for SSDI, you are at the bottom of the barrel."

As if the tapes in my head weren't loud enough, a successful businessman whom I knew from church accentuated my pain-filled conflict. "Four years ago I looked at your life and thought, *Here's a woman whose life is going nowhere.*" He continued, "Today I'd like your autograph." Ouch. I knew he was trying to give me a compliment, but all I heard was that somehow the past four years of my life had been a waste. It caused a logic-versus-emotions battle to erupt within. I knew those hidden years of obedience in the crucible of suffering were where God had honed my passions and molded a character of resilience. He had been preparing me for now, a time in His spotlight where He would creatively use me for His Kingdom work. But emotionally I was at the bottom of the barrel.

Success was stripping away my anonymity. People introduced me with words that sounded like those affiliated with a celebrity. "You may know Alice, the founder of HWI."

The responses included, "I've heard wonderful things about HWI. You helped our friends get bikes." Yet I didn't know how to resolve the painful dichotomy. HWI's success ignited an internal battle for me. *How can I be so successful and not hold down a paid position?*

From a medical standpoint, I wasn't aware of Dr. Benjamin Natelson's research about CFS. He had found a way to measure the problems that occur for CFS patients in the aftermath of physical exercise by doing an IQ test before a treadmill exercise test and immediately after. When a control subject (a person without CFS) used a treadmill, their IQ improved, but in individuals with CFS their IQs dropped twenty to thirty points. This explained why my ability to think or process information dropped dramatically after physical or mental exertion. Even after twenty-four hours, when a person with CFS retook the IQ test, their IQ drop persisted. The technical term for this devastating problem is post exertional malaise. It can last for twenty-four to seventy-two hours or more. Dr. Nancy Klimas, a leader in the field, remarked, "That's real! That's impressive! That's quantifiable!"[47]

When I shared my internal conflicts with my friend Jen, she said, "It's not right that you are unable to appreciate the fruit of your labor. It's time you seek help." Having been down a similar road a few times before in the past twenty years, I agreed to call a counselor for help. I couldn't afford to see a counselor, but I couldn't afford not to see one either. As usual, I was jumping ahead of God. All He wanted was for me to admit my need, follow His lead, and set up an appointment. Unable to reach Dr. David McKay, my former counselor, I called another psychologist, someone I had met months earlier at a party.

When talking with the psychologist on the phone, a deluge of questions swept over me. *Why can't I figure things out alone? Does seeking help indicate I've failed as a leader? Why can't I just get over it, drop it, and quit thinking that way?* Of course, I didn't voice these questions at the time. We ended the call by setting up an appointment to meet a week later.

While waiting to see the new psychologist, I wondered how things could appear so good and feel so bad. Did the media coverage over the last several months somehow mean I was becoming a prominent figure in my community? If so, I didn't want anyone to know I needed help. Somehow I was under the delusion that leaders aren't supposed to face any internal struggles.

During that week of waiting before the appointment, fuel was added to my fire when three Wheaton College students asked if they could interview me for a leadership class assignment. I lacked the strength, but I agreed. Somehow the students left the interview "inspired."

Later, in a class presentation, one said, "HWI doesn't just get from people; it also gives to those who give."

Another said, "Alice does not control people, but she is controlled by God to empower people."

The third said, "True leaders don't make people follow them. They make people want to follow because of their conviction or enthusiasm."

They summed up my style with a quote from John Maxwell, "The more people you develop, the greater the extent of dreams."[48]

These compliments brought tears to my eyes. Were they really talking about me?

Finally the day of my first counseling session arrived. The misinformation blaring in my head left me in turmoil.

The psychologist's first question was, "What brings you in to see me?"

All I could say was, "I can't figure out why I am so successful and can't hold down a job."

She asked, "What's your greatest fear right now? Are you afraid HWI will be taken from you?"

I snapped back, "No! No one wants HWI."

"Our job will be to try and find out what is disconnected," she told me. "We may uncover things you never knew were there." The truth is painful, and there is a price for freedom.

As the first session was drawing to a close, I informed the psychologist that I could afford four months of counseling. Inside all I wanted to do right then was bolt. I figured I'd set up our next appointment out of politeness and then cancel later in the week. But God had other plans.

After closing in prayer, she said to me, "This will be my contribution to your ministry. Your job is to commit to coming, accept it as a gift, not feel guilty, and think nothing more about it."

Later she said, "You didn't have a choice in my decision to provide free counseling, and furthermore, I really didn't either. The Holy Spirit prompted me to give, and I know His voice. When He leads, I'm to follow." So much for my plans to bolt!

When I left that first session, I couldn't figure out what I was afraid of, but the question opened the lock of my heart's door. My body was tremulous. I felt unglued and confused. I continued the day, scurrying around at a hurried pace, just trying to block out the pain bubbling up from deep within. But when night fell and I laid my head down, my heart was racing and my body ached. In prayer I cried out to God, asking Him to uncover the fears that had left me disconnected.

As those fears surfaced, I felt God reminding me of Joshua 1:9, the verse we'd chosen for HWI. "Have I not commanded you? Be strong and courageous. Do not be frightened, and do not be dismayed, for the LORD your God is with you wherever you go."[49]

During devotions the next day, I read the following Scripture: "The LORD was with [Joseph] and caused everything he did to succeed."[50] I went on to write this prayer in my journal: "As success keeps happening, help me to connect with it."

Soon afterward I felt challenged to consciously do three things: be present, let go of control, and keep my eyes open. I remembered how I longed for bicycle transportation to facilitate life transformation. But I hadn't considered that transformation needed to start within me, the leader.

A week later, before my second counseling session, a lightbulb shone on my deepest fear. *Are you afraid your health won't allow you to continue leading HWI?* Yes! Now I understood what the psychologist was asking during our first session. So I named that fear to God in prayer.

This brought back a memory from my first coast-to-coast trip. As our leader looked into his rearview mirror, he yelled, "Truck in front, truck in back," as two trucks barreled toward us on a one-lane highway. "DITCH IT! Get off the road!" I wondered, *Where to?* I needed to make a quick decision, and my only option was a precise ninety-degree turn up the front walkway to a stranger's house. The yard had a waist-high decorative chain-link fence around it. Maybe the owner had put it there as a polite "keep out" sign for an unwanted cycling visitor like me. But I couldn't believe how perfectly God had planned my exit. It saved me from becoming a semi sandwich!

By February 2007, another leader in my life, this time my psychologist, told me to "ditch it"—to take some time off from HWI. Indeed, it was wise counsel, because the fears had created a blind spot in my "mirror of life," causing me to lose perspective. I could tell my soul had an invisible chain-link fence around it, saying, "Keep out!" However, I knew if I wanted to continue finding and living out my God-given passions, I must take down the sign and face my fears.

The journey seemed as intrusive, foreign, and tricky now as it was back then, with just as sharp of a ninety-degree turn to navigate. But with the help of my counselor, the mighty Counselor, and others, I began to see past the blind spots. Only then could I let go of my perceived control of HWI and find safety as I returned to the walkway of my soul.

On a practical level, I also realized I needed to ditch it from HWI for the month of February. What that meant was that I told all five of my bike mechanics that we would not have any workdays for the month. I also told Kevin, our trike designer, that I would only be available to answer simple questions. I answered e-mails, but only to let people know I would deal with the issues in March. Doing so left me afraid that the forward momentum and rhythm we had built over the initial nineteen months would fall apart. But I needed to get off the road so God could show me things from my early childhood that were paralyzing me and creating ministry and leadership obstacles now.

One fear that surfaced came through a recurring nightmare of having my bike stolen, being taken captive, and losing my freedom. I had those nightmares when I was young, and now I was having them again. As I explored my fears, I discovered that I was afraid of having my passion for HWI stolen from me.

In the midst of these reflections, a question struck me. I wondered, *Who teaches us how to handle the complexities of success?* The concept was best illustrated in my own life on the same bicycle trip from more than thirty years ago.

The date was August 5, 1977. The place was Haystack Rock, at Cannon Beach, Oregon. The occasion was finishing my first coast-to-coast trip after forty-two days on the road. Hay Stack Rock didn't have a sign with a number, but in my brain the rock would always indicate mile marker 3,600, a trophy forever hung on my heart.

I was exhausted yet exhilarated as I dipped my front wheel into the Pacific Ocean. To finish the trip well required a time of reflection—basking in my achievement, acknowledging the courage and energy it took to complete my goal, and accepting the gift of accomplishment from God. I realized the trip had been life changing. My character had been molded by the journey as I rode, grew to know my teammates, encountered the locals, and contemplated the names on the historic site markers along the road. I had also experienced the power of what a team can accomplish when working together. We laughed while reminiscing about our "war stories"—the obstacles, detours, and difficulties that had threatened to steal our dreams and goals from us.

When I got home to Detroit, my coast-to-coast accomplishment created a problem that I couldn't identify then. Later, I would look back and realize I hadn't known how to handle the success of that trip. I wasn't prepared for the veil of my anonymity to be removed. Thus, it created much turmoil in my heart as I fielded the responses from others. For instance, "Wow, your parents really let you ride coast-to-coast at the age of fifteen? I would never have allowed my child to do that!" How was I to respond?

The comments baffled me as I sorted through my emotions, now mixed with extreme joy and sadness. Since I didn't want to provoke any jealous retorts from people, the only thing I knew how to do was undermine my success. When someone would say with great enthusiasm, "Oh, you biked cross-country?" I would shrug my shoulders and simply say yes, as if to communicate, *It's nothing special. Anyone could accomplish the same thing.*

On other occasions people announced my success in a way that made me out to be a hero. Still others wanted to live their lives vicariously through my victories, forgetting about all the hard work associated with them. It seemed that the mumbling and complaining associated with failure was more acceptable than sharing success.

Each time my cycling achievements were mentioned, I repelled the compliments in an attempt to obliterate my success from my thoughts, and conversations. But I couldn't. And now, all these years later, I still hadn't learned how to carry success.

During counseling, as I explored how I had handled success in the past, my eyes began to well up with tears. There was an acceptance/avoidance collision warring within. Over my lifetime I had believed a lie—that my giftedness was a curse. This lie had allowed me to repel and reject my success. I had formed a thick protective wall around my life, somehow setting me apart as abnormal. When someone would say, "You're way too hard on yourself," the words grieved me. I wondered, *Why am I so hard on myself?*

One day Harv, my Jewish friend, prefaced a compliment he was about to give me by saying, "I know your Christian answer will be that God gets the credit. It's okay if He gets the credit, but you deserve some too. It takes two to tango." His comment made me realize that others were watching my life. So far, I still hadn't done a good job defining, accepting, embracing, or properly celebrating the successes in my life. But I was determined to learn.

As I looked back over my life, I couldn't think of anyone in my family who had embraced their success or giftedness with love and gentleness. I was trapped behind the prison walls of that generational sin, unable to embrace the truths about my life. These walls hid my gentle spirit that longed for permission to embrace, accept, and celebrate my giftedness and internalize the truths others spoke into my life. So I prayed, confessed my sin, and asked God, "Break the generational curse over my life, which is rampant in my parents' generation, my generation, and the next generation after me. Give me insights and teach me to extend grace, peace, and love to myself. Help me to uncover the gifts in my own life."

It was then that I began the process of wisely handling success—a necessity for the health of HWI, others, and myself. I knew it was important to maintain humility while experiencing and celebrating success. But false humility, an old coping mechanism of mine, was no longer an option. I had to embrace my success now, as I had done back at Haystack Rock.

I wanted to use the words from Genesis as my model. When God finished forming creation, He "saw everything that he had made, and behold, it was very good."[51] Of course, I wasn't God, and my success would never be perfect, but it was still worth celebrating. But first I had to acknowledge that success doesn't just happen. I couldn't disown or deny the sheer determination, fortitude, discernment, discipline, energy, and sacrifice it took to get to the place of celebrating success.

I had to accept the accolades for daring to dream, overcoming fears, praying, listening to and obeying God's leading, and taking necessary action steps. Indeed, only God deserves all honor, glory, and praise, but celebrating was a way to acknowledge that He had given me my giftedness and successes, and He wanted me to live a contented life with them.

In June 2007, HWI was accomplishing yet another dream when I wrote out a check to buy bikes in Congo. I was reminded of the journey God had begun in 2005, when I met a Congolese pastor, his wife, and their two teenage sons. They brought up their need for bikes to facilitate ministry in a more efficient manner. At the time I was quick to clarify that we didn't have any money. The husband said, "We don't need money to talk and plan." He was right. As we began dialoguing, the wife shared the story of how important a bike was for her work.

"One day our church sent my husband and me to serve the Lord at another local church," she told me. "It was a thirty-minute-walk from our house. I began walking there three times a week to meet with the women, but soon I started having trouble with my legs. I prayed, 'God, I need a bicycle.'"

She decided that the only way to get enough money was to bake cakes and sell them to buy the bicycle. So she prayed again: "I need twenty-five kilograms of sugar so I can bake cakes."

She continued, "I took a few days and talked with God about the needs of my heart. The next day at church, our pastor prayed, 'God, give her what she needs, in Jesus' name.' After church my husband checked the mailbox. He brought an envelope and said, 'Here is the answer to our prayer.' We didn't know who sent it. God provided the money to buy everything for baking cakes."

She began baking cakes and buying one piece of the bicycle at a time until she got all the parts. The whole process took a year.

She never gave up, but instead was enchanted by each new part she gathered.

"Afterward I took it all to a mechanic, who put it together," she said. "I named the bicycle Dieudonne, meaning 'God gave.' Before riding, we dedicated the bicycle to God. Then I began using it to serve Him. When we left to spend two years in the United States, I wondered what I should do with this bicycle. Since God had given it to me for His work, I decided I must give it away, so it would continue serving Him. I gave it to a committed pastor's wife who teaches women in Napopo Bible Institute."

When I handed the couple the check, the wife jumped with joy. She said, "He has returned to me over ten times what I've given. This is an amazing miracle. In my heart, I know God is alive." Afterward we dedicated the work to God in prayer through jubilant celebration and great anticipation of what God had planned.

"Thank you, Lord, for blessing our obedience," the husband concluded.

My joyous celebration ended abruptly when I returned home and found my back door wide open and shattered glass on the floor. "I've been robbed!" I cried in shock and disbelief. Then I called the police. When I looked around my home, I saw that my bedroom had been ransacked. They had stolen all my gold and pearl jewelry—even my priceless gold chain and bicycle pendant! My heart was crushed. What a heinous crime. They probably got pennies for my priceless pendant. But they couldn't steal the love, the sentiment, or the promise that pendant represented.

After the police left, I called the Congolese family. The four of them came right over, sharing one of their rich cultural practices of sitting with a person in grief and comforting them. They reminded me that the burglary couldn't steal the joy of what God was doing around the world through HWI. I made a conscious choice not to give the thieves power to steal my joy and rob me of embracing and celebrating success. Not now, and not later!

I was learning that just as people can't enter into our suffering and deepest pain, the same is true with success and feelings of joy. These are things we fully experience with God alone. But to continue making room in my soul for embracing and celebrating success would mean aligning myself with those who would join me in the celebration. With the Lord as the anchor of my life, I didn't have to allow circumstances, situations, or people to devastate or destroy me anymore.

For years I'd prayed for healing. God was answering from the inside out. He wanted transformation to begin in my heart so He could give me *shalom*—"not only 'peace' but also tranquility, safety, well-being, welfare, health, contentment, success, comfort, wholeness, and integrity."[52] Only then could I participate in genuine, vibrant, transforming ministry, crossing cultural barriers as I invited others to dare to embark on their unique dream-filled adventure too.

The Power of Drafting

I was in for another surprise in 2007. This one involved BJ, a member of my church who lived with Down syndrome. He would become a key player in making dreams come true through our trike program.

Since BJ loved bikes, he had volunteered the previous summer during some of our mechanic workdays. As volunteers arrived, he greeted each with a handshake and a sincere, joy-filled hello. Then BJ would spend the day sorting parts, cleaning bikes, and airing up tires using our powered compressor.

After his work was finished, BJ would reward himself by taking our hand-pedaled trike for a ride. Due to balance issues, he wasn't able to shed his bicycle training wheels until he was sixteen years old. Thus, he understood better than anyone else on our team the value of making adaptations and alterations so those with disabilities could pedal a trike and experience the freedom it offered.

One day when BJ's mother picked him up, he said to her, "Take the trike to the Joni and Friends retreat!" JNF is an international disability ministry that was founded in 1979 by Joni Eareckson Tada. In 1967, at the age of seventeen, a diving accident had left Joni a quadriplegic, confined to a wheelchair and unable to use her hands. However, through her life-altering circumstances, Joni surrendered herself and her situation to God. After two years of rehabilitation, she was determined to use what she had learned through her disability to help others in similar situations.[53]

BJ's comment was music to my ears. I had dreamed for more than twenty years of one day meeting Joni. I had read most of her books and thought highly of her life and ministry. In fact, the book I had been reading the night before I met the Lutembekas in 2003, when I had told God all the good ideas were gone, was one of hers. What struck me then with fresh insight was that Joni and I both had a disability. Somehow God was using her disability in a dynamic Kingdom way, and I wanted the same for my life.

Now BJ and I shared the same dream. We at HWI wanted to give individuals with disabilities an opportunity to try our trikes, and the JNF retreat provided such a venue. The program was flexible and designed to provide time together for families who live with disabilities. I didn't have any connections with JNF, but BJ did! His mom served on Chicago's JNF board of directors.

In June 2007, we headed off to the JNF retreat, which was held at a conference center in the beautiful resort town of Syracuse, Indiana, off Lake Wawasee, the largest natural lake in Indiana. Our week there was such a big hit for the attendees that the JNF team asked if we would leave the trikes another week for the second session. The JNF retreat was beneficial for us, as well. It allowed us to see the strengths and weaknesses of our design as people with a wide variety of disabilities rode the trikes.

Watching BJ show others how to ride the trikes was inspiring. He encouraged them to try something new, overcoming their fears to reach a seemingly impossible dream. As I watched BJ serve the Lord in this way, it reminded me of an important bicycle skill known as drafting.

Drafting occurs when a group of cyclists ride single or double file behind each other in a "pace line." The group is known as a peloton. The peloton leader, the rider in front, does the hard work, breaking the wind, which is tiring and requires extra strength. The job of each person behind the leader in the peloton is to position their front wheel about a bike length behind the back wheel of the rider in front of them, without touching or overlapping tires. If a larger gap forms between bikes, the rider who has fallen behind has to work twice as hard to break the wind.

However, if the rider overlaps tires, it leaves that cyclist unable to control his or her bike and susceptible to a single or multiple bike pile-up—and potentially serious injuries.

An experienced peloton looks simple and graceful. But it took me almost my entire first coast-to-coast trip to understand the concept or value of a peleton. Learning to maintain the proper position within the line required skill, concentration, and cooperation. Maintaining a proper cadence, rhythm, focus, and precision were all skills I had to learn before I could apply them within my peloton. Proper pace line etiquette included keeping our heads up and alerting each other to upcoming dangers, turns, and moves. This is done by calling out things like, "Rock right," "Car rear," "Hole in front," "Turning right," and "Passing on the left."

The golden rule of a pace line is that the leader cannot go faster than the slowest rider. Weaker riders are positioned in the middle of the pack, so they glean the greatest benefit from the stronger riders. When the lead rider gets tired, he or she drops to the back of the pack, allowing the next person to lead, thus dispersing the workload. Riding in an effective peloton provides team camaraderie.

In 1977, after five days of demoralizing twenty to thirty mile per hour gusting headwinds along the Columbia River Gorge, our entire team of sixty riders formed a peloton. It was eight riders across and eight rows deep. Since I was one of the weakest riders, I was positioned in the middle of the last row. Even so I was pedaling with difficulty in the easiest gear, as if I were climbing the steepest mountain. But I couldn't imagine the ride without the other fifty-nine riders in front of me, pulling me in their draft.

Now my greatest weakness, my disability, made it such that the Lord would need to be our peloton leader. Once again I was reminded that if we were going to ride into the great unknown, I had to rely on the strengths, talents, and resources of those in HWI's peloton to go the distance. BJ was out in front now, leading our team with his talents and resources. None of us had BJ's strengths, so we needed him to take us through this leg of the journey. I couldn't do BJ's job, nor could he do mine. But as part of the same peloton, while following God, we were able to participate in seeing trikes used in yet another way as tools for expanding His Kingdom.

The wife of a participant at the retreat said, "I haven't seen my husband so excited since his accident four years ago." When we met another young man, who was paralyzed on his right side, I asked, "Do you want to try the trike?"

His shoulders slouched. "I can't do it," he said. With help and encouragement from BJ and the rest of our team, he tried. The next day he returned with friends, and with a big smile on his face, he rode off on the trike again.

Another family at the retreat said, "You have made our daughter Anika so happy this week. We can't thank you enough."

Anika was an eight-year-old, adopted from Belarus at the age of four. When her parents had gone to Belarus on a mission trip, adoption wasn't part of their itinerary. Until they met Anika. When Anika saw her future mom and dad, she ran into her mom's arms saying, "Mama." That surprise greeting forever changed their lives.

When Anika arrived in the United States, she walked off the plane, and four months later she walked into the hospital for surgery. But due to complications during surgery, she left a paraplegic. Her life would never be the same again. Still, it couldn't steal her determination, athleticism, or charm.

On the first day of the JNF retreat, during free time activities, Anika showed up first. After her dad lifted her onto the trike, we gave her a few quick lessons. Then her dad walked alongside her while she began to get the hang of riding the trike, which didn't take long. She picked up momentum with each pedal stroke, her hair blew in the wind, and a smile engulfed her face with the thrill of riding.

I expected that her trike ride would last about five to ten minutes and then she'd take off for the next free-time activity. It didn't happen. She came back and wanted to try another trike. Anika tried all three of our trikes that day, riding for two hours. Of course, like any rider, she took a few much-needed breaks—sitting on the trike, eating cotton candy, or having a drink to refuel. But then she was off again.

At lunch on Tuesday her dad said, "We won't see you today. We are going water tubing." Forty-five minutes after free-time activities began, there was Anika. She had her bathing suit on and was dripping wet from tubing, but she was raring to ride. She rode for over an hour, until free time ended.

On Wednesday her dad said, "Anika won't be there today. She is going horseback riding." Again, around the same time, who rolled up eager to ride but Anika.

And so it went. Each lunch hour I heard the same line, but each day Anika rushed through her special free-time activity and returned to ride the trikes. By the end of the week she had spent eight hours riding our trikes.

"She has Olympic potential," a physical therapist stated.

When Kevin, our trike designer, came one day to glean insight about the engineering changes that were needed, he saw Anika ride. I mentioned the possibility of building a junior hand-cycle racer for her. Anika worked the same charm on Kevin that she had worked on her parents years earlier in Belarus. She melted Kevin's heart too.

As I reflected back over the year, I realized how important it was for me to have passed through all the mile markers since 1992 to accept my own disability. If I hadn't done so, I probably wouldn't have been sensitive to BJ's dreams and determination to give others with disabilities the opportunity to experience the freedom of pedaling a bike or a trike. The gifts of those living with a disability are often overlooked because they are harder to uncover or implement. Yet an inherent ingredient of personal dignity is the opportunity to participate in something meaningful— something that provides purpose and a sense of belonging.

The experience of letting BJ lead helped me see that there were times when I didn't slow down as a leader to make room for the gifts of other team members. As a result, I violated the golden rule of team riding—not going faster than the slowest rider. At times, under the guise of having too much to do, I rationalized my disrespectful actions by thinking I was the strongest rider and that the one lagging behind required too much work for me to wait. But BJ's leadership helped me to see how important the unique gifts of each team member are in their perfect place and time.

If I had rushed ahead of God's plan, I would have undermined BJ's dignity and overlooked his gifts—and all for the sake of completing my agenda. I learned an important lesson about honoring all members of the body of Christ as image bearers, partners together in Kingdom work. I hoped I'd never forget that each member can give and receive from HWI at the same time.

Throughout the summer and fall, Kevin designed and built a racing trike for Anika. The trike was aerodynamic, high-tech, and multiple-geared and would allow Anika to work toward her ultimate athletic potential. With Anika in mind, Kevin named it Scirocco, which meant "African wind."

Months later, when we fitted Anika to Scirocco, she rode around, smiling and singing, "I'm having so much fun." She left everyone who tried to run alongside her in the dust.

Kevin watched with excitement as he did some of his final engineering analysis. Afterward he said, "I have found what I was created to do."

Then and there our dream for a junior hand-cycle racing team was born. Where it would lead us, only God knew.

Stops along the Way

As 2007 came to a close, I found another small black velvet box—this one under the Christmas tree. I had an inkling what was inside, given that six months earlier my bicycle necklace had been stolen when my house was broken into. But that didn't stop the tingling feeling rising from my heart when I laid my eyes on the gift. This time it was handed to me by another special person. He was as excited to give me the present as I was to accept it.

When I cracked open the box, I saw something gold and round. I took it out and upon further inspection found a delicate bicycle pendant with wheels that turned. As I looked up at my nephew, Ben, HWI's "co-director," there was a sparkle in my eyes and a huge grin on my face, which he mirrored back to me.

This time it wasn't just my brother who picked out my pendant; a dynamic father-son duo had done it together. My original bike pendant, accompanied by a bike store promise, had been tweaked by the Lord. This necklace was a rolling symbol of my "spiritual bike shop," as Harv called HWI. Now my professional speaking attire was complete, accessorized with a new pendant hanging from a gold chain. Of the more than two hundred bicycles that came onto my property that year, the best by far was the one waiting for me under the Christmas tree. God would use that bike, along with the others, to continue weaving His plans through His Wheels.

Yet by the beginning of 2008, the continuous activity related to the bikes and trikes had caused a personal problem. Now my adrenaline was stuck in high gear. It was as if a constant tidal wave were rushing through my body and there was no way to switch it off. My brain kept churning out information. When I lay down to pray, it sounded like an explosion was rumbling through my ears. My body trembled like the ocean floor. Worst of all, I had no idea how to rectify the problem.

The adrenaline rush continued until June, when I had the opportunity to attend a weeklong ministry leadership retreat with Carolyn, a missionary friend from Ethiopia. There I realized just how fatigued I was on all fronts. During devotions one day, the text from the early part of Elijah's ministry resonated with me.

> *The word of the* LORD *came to [Elijah]: "Depart from here and turn eastward and hide yourself by the brook Cherith."* . . . *The ravens brought him bread and meat in the morning, and bread and meat in the evening, and he drank from the brook.* . . . *Then the word of the* LORD *came to him, "Arise, go to Zarephath."* [64]

After reading and meditating on these words, I wrote out the following prayer. "I want my life as a leader to be an empty canvas on which God can create a masterpiece that displays His signature."[55] At the time I didn't really know what people meant when they said, "Watch out for what you pray for!" But I was soon to find out.

An unexpected invitation came from Carolyn three months later. She had since moved to Florida and invited me to visit her there from the middle of December to the middle of January 2009. I knew my body needed rest, and my accountability partners encouraged me to go. So I booked a flight, eager to get some rest and relaxation. But this was not just a vacation. It would require me to implement one of the hardest spiritual disciplines for me—letting go.

As I prepared to leave for Florida, I reflected back on all that had transpired within HWI. Kevin, our trike designer/engineer, had built twelve different trike prototypes, along with four assembly fixtures. Since the fixtures could rotate 360 degrees on a stand, such latitude of adjustability would accommodate both the able and the disabled in the trike manufacturing process. The fixtures would provide greater building accuracy and efficiency.

Throughout 2008, trikes went out to Senegal, West Africa, and Bulgaria. Dawn Clark, the disability ministry leader from College Church, described how the trike was used as a tool for expanding Christ's Kingdom among their short-term mission team in Bulgaria. The team went to teach Bulgarian leaders about disability ministries. "As we started to unpack the trike [at a nursing home-type setting]," Dawn said, "a master mechanic, born without legs, came to check it out and took charge of putting the trike together. With great delight he hopped onto the trike and started putting it through its paces, which included a trip to a nearby café."

This trike helped the team establish credibility for their week of ministry to the disabled. Near the end of the week, the local TV station filmed the mechanic riding the trike. The interviewer asked why they had come. Dawn said, "We wanted the disabled to know that God has not forgotten them and that He loves them, and so do we."

On the bike side of our ministry, we had distributed 516 bicycles in two years. Of those, sixty-six crossed oceans, making their way to Congo, Togo, Tanzania, and Angola. The rest were distributed in the United States to individuals affiliated with twenty different ministries and organizations.

By take-off time for my month of rest in Florida, HWI was moving at a ferocious pace. I felt somewhat like the prophet Elijah, steeped in the height of ministry. In the Scripture account I'd read, Elijah had just revealed to King Ahab that a three-year drought was coming. For me, the challenge was knowing that while I was gone, Kevin would have to make sure a trike got off to Angola, Africa, without my assistance. But God wanted me to follow Elijah's example—to get away and go to my "brook Cherith" in Florida.

Since my round-trip flight was already booked, I figured that, unlike Elijah, I had an ending date to plug into my computerized calendar. He was just told his departure date and where to go. And as Elijah came to his complete ministry stop, I read how God took care of his every need.

As I read more about Elijah's life, I could see that God had him stop at Cherith in preparation for the big events awaiting him. One such event was when he built an altar, soaked the sacrificial bull in a pool of water, and then prayed for the Lord God to light the fire as a way of showing the 450 Baal worshipers that he served the true God. And God honored Elijah's obedience. As I pondered Elijah's story, I couldn't help but wonder if God was asking me to stop now so He could prepare me for even bigger things through HWI. If so, I couldn't imagine things getting any bigger!

Now during the first few days in Florida, I found myself slowing down. I recognized how jittery and jumpy my body was from sheer physical exhaustion. In addition, I was experiencing irregular breathing patterns, also common with CFS. I was afraid to switch off my energy completely, because I was afraid that when I tried turning the power switch back on, it wouldn't work. I would describe my physical energy the way some of my African friends described their electricity in remote villages. "We have intermittent power," they told me. "We can't depend on it, but we are grateful when it works, even for an hour or two." I can't say, however, that I was quite as content with my intermittent physical energy as they were with their electrical energy.

I was reminded of a cycling scenario I'd been guilty of many times in the past when approaching a stop sign, especially on a deserted road. I'd slow down, make a quick glance both ways, and resume my normal pedaling cadence. It is easy to justify and rationalize a rolling stop, as opposed to a complete stop. After all, I thought, I could see over the cars from my bike. It took less energy to slow down, and it didn't create such a disruption in pedaling cadence, thus making it easier on my leg muscles. Besides, making a complete stop would have required me to remove my shoes from the clipless pedals, and restarting would involve clipping back into the pedals, rebalancing on the bike, and expending a blast of energy to regain speed.

However, a rolling stop is dangerous because a cyclist glances both ways but may not see the driver waiting at the stop sign. The driver, having arrived at the stop sign first, has the right of way but is skittish to proceed because the cyclist isn't following the rules of the road, thus heightening the chances of a bicycle-car casualty. Also, pedestrians crossing the street may be left wondering if they can safely cross, as the green light indicates, without getting hit by the bike.

As I considered this idea of stopping, I was also reminded of a question that often slipped out of people's mouths over the years when I told about my cross-country trips.

"Do you ride across the country without stopping to sleep?" people frequently asked.

The challenge of bicycling coast-to-coast seemed mind boggling and exhausting enough in itself. But not even stopping to sleep? That was unfathomable!

At the beginning of most days the unsolved mystery was where we would sleep that night. Wandering Wheels had about six preplanned stops at churches along the road, complete with potluck dinners. Most days we were happy if there was an outside shower in the form of a green garden hose. But that didn't stop me from hoping each day that we would end up at a five-star stop, complete with indoor plumbing, showers, air conditioning, and carpeted floors. I'll never forget one such five-star stop during my second trip, when we stayed at the Virginia Military Institute. In addition to having plenty of showers, they also had an adequate sized water heater, so we all got hot showers that night.

If someone had asked if I had done the HWI journey without stopping since 2005, I would have had to say, with the exception of a few ordered health stops, "Yes! Guilty as charged!" Just as I wasn't expected to ride coast-to-coast without stopping, the same was true of my journey as the executive director of HWI.

Even so, I found myself bargaining with God. *Wouldn't it be okay if I made a rolling stop through my time in Florida?* Deep inside, however, I knew a complete stop was required.

I tried to rationalize being so engrossed in ministry that I didn't want to stop. My idea deteriorated as I remembered how engrossed I had been in my bicycle trips. No one saw the stops on my bike trips as a waste of time and energy. Quite the opposite. These times were seen as opportunities to allow the body to recharge and heal from the strain of such a grueling trip.

So now I had to wonder what real issues were really preventing me from stopping. I realized it was easier to keep going, living off the adrenaline of ministry and hiding my vulnerabilities. Stopping was dangerous, because that was when the Lord could examine and expose my soul issues, which was often a painful process.

Donald Barnhouse offers this insight: "Never grow weary of the leading of the Lord, for impatience is denial of

His wisdom. Not only your steps but your stops are ordered by Him."[56]

After a few short days in Florida, when the adrenaline fix had dried up, my body let down, and exhaustion made it impossible to maintain a clear emotional perspective. The victories of accomplishment from the past three years of ministry eluded me. Instead, the temptations of defeat and spiritual discouragement overwhelmed me, causing me to mope around and crumple into a pity party. *Doesn't God understand I'm an executive director of a growing Christian organization?* I wondered, *How will I regain the volunteer momentum for HWI if I'm away for a month?*

What I didn't know then was that I would have fifteen weeks spread out over the next year to obey God with complete ministry stops. I'm glad I didn't get a memo with all those dates at once, because it was hard enough right then to stop for four weeks.

I remembered a stop sign I had run back in 1977, at the age of fifteen, just before taking off for my first cross-country trip. It was the first weekend my parents had ever left me home alone. Their only instruction was, "Don't ride your bike to your youth leader's house." They were concerned about my safety, which was legitimate, but I was bored and lonely, and the weather was wonderful for cycling. So on Saturday around noon, I set off for the thirteen-mile, sixty-minute bike ride to my youth leader's home.

I lived off 6 Mile Road, on Detroit's east side. My leader's house was in a western suburb of Detroit, which required riding almost ten miles on 8 Mile Road, an east-west artery. This road divided Detroit from thirteen suburban communities to the south, and according to some estimates, it averaged seventy thousand cars a day. On top of that, this part of the city has been described as "a grim parade along the south side of the road" composed of "Detroit's destitute and drug-addled."[57]

I made it to my leader's home safely, but I felt guilty for disobeying my folks the whole time I was there. In the late afternoon, as I mounted my bike to head home, a dark, ominous storm cloud loomed overhead. With no time to waste, I shifted into high gear in the hope of racing out the storm and arriving home before my family pulled in from their Chicago trip. But five miles from home, thunder and lightning came crashing down, along with a deluge of rain. It wasn't going to stop my race if I had any say in the matter.

So I continued on home, now having made the bright decision to get off the busy 8 Mile road and onto a parallel sidewalk. At the same time I approached an intersection. There I met a driver who planned to occupy the same space as my bike at the exact same time. He didn't see me, so I hit the brakes. They didn't work! *Now what?* With only a split second to make a decision, I tried to turn in the same direction as the car, hoping to avoid a collision. We sideswiped, which caused me to crash, leaving a sizable dent in his car and resulting in a bruised-up knee and twisted handlebars for me. The driver got out to make sure I was okay, and he left just as quickly.

Since there was no one to call, I continued riding home, shaking from the cold rain, the wreck, and the knowledge that there was no way to keep my lie quiet. My youth leader, my parents, the owner of the car, and I were all impacted by my wrongful actions. Now in retrospect I could see that my parents knew best when they had asked me to obey their stop sign all those years ago.

Back in Florida, despite my concerns about stopping, I had to remind myself that God knew best. I tried to heed His rules for my ministry road, recognizing there was a benefit to getting away from my ministry base to be still and truly know God.[58]

While in Florida, I stayed at the missionary retirement village where Carolyn worked. However, I wasn't prepared for the barrage of questions I would face. "How can you spend a month just stopping?" "Are you independently wealthy?" "What do you do for a living?" "Who do you work for?" "How can you sit in the house all day?" "Aren't you bored?" "What are you doing while you are here?" The frequency of the questions reinforced that coming to a complete ministry stop is a foreign concept.

It's no wonder why. Stopping pierced my soul as it gave the right of way to loneliness and isolation. As the need to justify my actions surfaced, I was forced to observe what was happening in my heart and listen to God. When I couldn't defend myself, I felt judged as insignificant because of the appearance of being unproductive, with nothing to show for my obedience.

Part of me wished I could run away from the feelings and avoid the work God wanted to do in my life. As I continued my soul search, I asked myself, "Are my importance and self-esteem linked to my performance?" "What accolades am I looking for?" "Do I have to tell people that I'm exhausted and cantankerous and to stay out of my way?" Through further exploration, I realized that my leadership role gave me a sense of purpose and made me feel indispensable.

Stepping away from the hectic pace of ministry was the first step in self-care, a responsibility Scripture speaks about. "Do you not know that you are God's temple and that God's Spirit dwells in you? If anyone destroys God's temple, God will destroy him. For God's temple is holy, and you are that temple."[59] Next I needed to silence the blaring distractions by turning off my cell phone, shutting down the Internet, resting, and spending time with God. There I found myself in the Lord's crucible, acknowledging that I'd snatched control of HWI away from Him, confessing my repeated sins of fear and guilt, and ultimately receiving God's forgiveness.

The process of letting go of the everyday worries took about three weeks. Then I could still my heart and listen to God while pondering life, regrouping, and allowing my imagination to soar. As my time was freed from interfacing with society, I was able to devote myself to solitude and prayer until the creative ministry juices started flowing again.

While I was tucked away from ministry, God was orchestrating His plans around the world. When I returned from my first month away, an unexpected opportunity awaited me. HWI was asked to send a trike with a missionary team going to Haiti. In doing so, we were also able to do some more field testing. When the Haiti team returned, I was humbled to read the account of the trike recipient.

Prior to receiving the trike, Maxene [a twenty-six-year-old] had believed his paralysis was the result of a voodoo spell. When he saw the trike, his face lit up. The team told him it was a gift from God, and one of the members of the team followed up with this prayer: "God's power is greater than any other power. Even over the roughest road, he can smooth it out."

Maxene did not have any trouble negotiating the rocky, rut-filled, impossible-looking terrain on crutches, and he didn't have any trouble with the trike either. As he rode away, practically in tears, with a smile beaming across his face, the team could tell he was experiencing a new kind of freedom. "For the rest of my life, I can never repay you for what you have done," he stated.

For the first time ever, he was able to get down to the river, where the locals bathe, by himself. The team's prayer is that through a relationship with the pastor, Maxene will begin traveling the path toward true freedom and hope in Jesus Christ. One of the team members said that delivering the trike "was a blessing and highlight of my trip. Maxene has now witnessed the power of a loving God to help dispel the darkness of Voodoo worship that paralyzed his spiritual life."

Maxene wrote, "I praise the Lord for you. God has used you to help me and to bring such a souvenir in my life. I had nobody, but God put me in your heart. What a gift! I will never stop thanking you and I will never stop glorifying the name of the Lord for this awesome gift. Now I need to go to church to praise Him. I know God will finish what he has already started. With Jesus nothing shall be impossible."

I realized only God could have orchestrated such an ideal partnership.

Just prior to leaving for my second month off, I met an indigenous missionary sent out from Uganda to Rwanda. There, only months earlier, he had begun Dayspring Primary School in Kigali. He said, "Bicycles would facilitate transportation for the employees. As a benefit option, they could receive a bicycle on a loan basis, having a small amount deducted from their wages, which would also provide employee stability for the school. Through the repayment plan, the school could continue the bicycle program."

While I was away in Florida for my second month, HWI continued forward. Kevin, our engineer, met with the missionary from Uganda for about twenty hours, showing him how to build a trike and teaching him all the skills and tools needed for prototyping. Only God could have orchestrated such an ideal opportunity for Kevin, the son of an industrial arts teacher. The missionary learned how to bend metal trike tubes, weld, work with fiberglass, use basic hand tools, and operate machine tools for metal and wood work. The two of them also toured an industrial metal parts fabrication company, and the missionary learned to navigate Auto Cad, a computer drafting program. When he returned to Rwanda, HWI bought him a copy of Auto Cad to use as he began his technical training program.

Several months later, the missionary wrote, "HWI has set 'bicycle fire' to the school. Our teachers are exceedingly happy for the bicycle loan plan. Four of the staff have received brand-new bikes. I believe this loan plan will promote our vision of excellent child education by stabilizing the school as the teaching staff concentrate on the children."

Meanwhile, during my time in Florida, I'd been talking to Carolyn's dad, Dr. Adolph, the head of Soddo Christian

Hospital in Ethiopia. I began dreaming about ways to get trikes there too. Throughout the next year it seemed like our "impossible" dream would never become a reality. God had other plans, but He wasn't in quite the hurry we were to unveil them.

At the beginning of May 2009, I returned from Florida to celebrate HWI's fourth birthday with four faithful mechanics. They reminded me that we had given away over a thousand bicycles—ten times more than my initial dream. We had distributed 120 bicycles internationally by then, and we were on our second production run of forty trikes. In addition, we had just added a volunteer accountant to our team roster.

I was learning that as I continued to lead from a place of need, Christ would remain in charge of HWI—and of my life, too.

Moving Down the Road

In September 2009, on yet another return flight from Florida to Illinois, I engaged in conversation with the lawyer sitting next to me. She gave a raving review of Malcolm Gladwell's book *Outliers: The Story of Success*. My curiosity was piqued by the thesis: it takes ten thousand hours of practice to make a prodigy. So I got the book and began reading. After finishing the first chapter, I went to prayer. The Lord challenged me to become a "prayer prodigy." By then I was comfortable praying one to two hours a day and had seen the amazing results of God's divine orchestrations.

But I wasn't sure about this new idea. Out of shock, I repeated the challenge out loud: "Pray ten thousand hours. Pray 10K!" I wondered, *How long would it take? What would the commitment entail? What would I have to give up to reach the goal? How many hours are in a year? A week?*

The next morning I calculated the hours: 24 in a day, 168 in a week, 720 in a month, and 8,760 in a year. It was going to be a long journey. As an athlete, I knew that if I was going to enter training and take my skill to another level, I needed a plan and a strategy. I first had to ask myself, "Am I willing to invest and seek hard after my goal?" Simultaneously I wondered if I could get out of Pray 10K, because it sounded like an impossible idea.

Since I couldn't see the end of the goal, I wasn't sure I wanted to venture down the road by faith. However, a quote by Herbert Lockyer gave my prayer journey perspective: "Holy men of old came boldly before God believing that prayer was 'the slender nerve that moveth the muscles of Omnipotence.'"[60] I wanted what Lockyer described.

But I also knew prayer is the hardest terrain to traverse, wrestling "against the rulers, against the authorities, against the cosmic powers over this present darkness, against the spiritual forces of evil in the heavenly places."[61] It was also something that lasted into eternity. "While bodily training is of some value, godliness is of value in every way, as it holds promise for the present life and also for the life to come."[62]

So now I had to make a plan, the initial components of which included clocking my prayer hours, letting my accountability partners know of my goal, and beginning an intensive prayer journal. I knew this challenge would require concentrated effort and lifestyle changes. I would have to decrease the time I spent on the phone, watching TV, and searching the Internet. I prayed, "May I understand that I am not giving something up. Instead, help me to see that storehouses of blessings are mine."

The first discoveries I made were that intelligent prayer requires work, study, research, and the Holy Spirit's direction. If I wanted my prayer life to grow in maturity, I needed to apply the following scriptural principle: "He set himself to seek God in the days of Zechariah, who instructed him in the fear of God, and as long as he sought the LORD, God made him prosper."[63]

Pray 10K! It struck me that I had bicycled ten thousand miles by the age of thirty. This challenge wasn't a coincidence. When I considered the adventures I had experienced by bike, I now had the same giddy excitement, trepidation, and invigoration, laced with fear. It caused me to pray, asking God to expand my spiritual journey as He performed His mighty deeds.

I couldn't wait to see the mountains God would move through this prayer journey. If the view from God's outdoor cathedral was breathtaking by bike, I could only imagine the grandeur from a prayer peak.

Where would Pray 10K take me? It was mind-boggling to consider the dangers and the stamina needed for such an intense journey. I wondered, *What will it cost? Who will I meet along the way? What is the itinerary? Will I make it? What suffering will I endure? What joys will I experience? How did I conjure up such a cockamamie idea?*

As I thought of embarking on my Pray 10K journey, I was transported back to my second coast-to-coast trip from San Diego, California, to Virginia Beach, Virginia, when I was sixteen. As I registered and trained for the trip, I was fired up and raring to go. When I dreamed about the previous trip I'd taken, I had selective memory. I only remembered how amazing it was to have gone across the country the first time.

But the night before we were to mount our bikes, heading out of San Diego, my emotions skipped a few gears. I wondered if I'd lost my mind by signing up to take a second trip. The realities of the difficult days and the exhaustion that accompanied riding a hundred miles a day on the first trip were now stampeding over all my wonder-filled memories.

I wanted to tell the leaders that I had made a mistake and ask if they'd let me fly home on the next plane headed to Detroit. I didn't think I had it in me to go cross-country again. But I didn't have the guts to tell the leaders. I knew it wouldn't get me anywhere anyway. A mental and emotional battle ensued, vying for my allegiance. "I can do it," I declared while exhaling the statement. But the next inhalation was filled with a gasp of fear: "I'll never make it. Just let me quit now before I even start."

As I began Pray 10K a volunteer told me how another ministry leader had driven more than three thousand miles throughout the county, looking for free warehouse space. As I pondered the story, I calculated that he was aimlessly wandering for at least a hundred hours. Since my four-year-old car at the time only had seventeen thousand miles on it (driving was difficult for my health), that was not a viable plan for me to pursue.

But we desperately needed space. It was our fourth year of ministry, and the headquarters remained my home, with more than two hundred bikes sprawled out in my backyard. Such a scene was creating a social dilemma, tempting the neighborhood youth to steal. In addition, my garage was bursting at the seams with five trikes, manufacturing fixtures, and pieces of steel. Our second production run of forty trike part kits was about to be completed. As my team anticipated the completion of the parts, they kept asking, "Where are we going to store them?" I didn't have an answer. I knew we needed some warehouse space. But where were we to go? How would we afford rent?

I decided that the best way for me to clock a hundred hours searching for space was in prayer, trusting the Lord to provide. Whenever I shared my Pray 10K dream and my plan to look for space, I did so with a sheepish tone, knowing the road ahead seemed ludicrous. The same emotional war ensued in my head now as it had in 1978, on the verge of heading off into the great unknown of another bike trip. Yet the Bible says, "All things, whatsoever ye shall ask in prayer, believing, ye shall receive."[64]

During the first couple of weeks of my Pray 10K journey, I had the stamina to sign up for the adventure of prayer and test it out. But soon I wondered, *How will prayer help me find space?* I felt desperate and went looking for property in an industrial park, only three miles southeast of my home. I parked in front of a "For Rent" sign and prayed. "Lord, You know we need space." Afterward I was reminded of my prayer plan and went home and continued praying.

A week later I took my friend Carolyn, who was in town for a visit, to see the space. This time I wrote down the phone number. But once again I had to return home and continue praying. Then, on October 31, four weeks after starting my Pray 10K journey, while at a block party, I began talking with a neighbor. I told him about HWI and our need for space.

"I'm a pilot," the neighbor said, "and I have space in my airplane hangar, about twenty-three miles west of here. You can use it for free."

I left the party elated. Here was a powerful prayer discovery for me, after seventy hours of prayer. I jotted down this sentence in my journal: "God is a loose cannon of creativity, which when directed by the winds of the Holy Spirit can provide a great adventure."

As I began to share the story with people, I had an ever-increasing sense of confidence and excitement about my new journey. I found myself concurring with Martin Luther's discovery: "If I fail to spend two hours in prayer each morning, the devil gets the victory through the day. I have so much business I cannot get on without spending three hours daily in prayer."[65]

By the hangar moving day in late November, I had prayed 110 hours. I was stunned and speechless. God's timing was perfect. The hangar was climate controlled so our trike inventory wouldn't rust, and it was furnished with a TV lounge, a refrigerator, a workshop, and a bathroom. It all seemed surreal.

Around the same time, Kevin and I began to talk with Ken, a missionary kid who had grown up in Sierra Leone, about the possibility of Ken joining HWI's board. I had met Ken and his family in 2006 after they returned from serving for ten years in Guinea, West Africa. HWI had given them bikes. Since Ken had mechanical knowledge and missionary experience, we had asked for his professional insights on the first generation of our present overseas trike design.

As we talked now, it became clear that God's plans were different from ours. Ken had the skills to become our trike division coordinator. It would begin as a paid contractor position, at ten hours a week, with the hope that one day it would grow into a full-time position. I had no idea where the finances would come from, but as the board and I continued praying, we began talking about having Ken join us in a consulting role. I kept thinking, *God, You want me to do what? Are You out of Your mind?* While questioning God, I became aware of how scared I was to take the faith leap.

A month later I returned to Florida. Two days before Christmas, my friend and I drove to I-TEC (Indigenous People's Technology and Education Center), founded by Steve Saint. I-TEC's mission is to help indigenous churches in their journey toward independence by enabling them to overcome the technological and educational hurdles that stand in their way. They equip people around the world with the necessary technology and train them so they can care for themselves with minimal outside support.

When Steve saw a picture of HWI's trike, he shared a heart-breaking story. He said, "While serving as a missionary in Mali, West Africa, I saw what looked like a small animal crawling along in sewer water. When I got closer, I was appalled to find a small child pulling himself along by his hands." Steve encouraged us, "Keep doing what you are doing," and he and his staff offered to help HWI by sharing their expertise.

I-TEC shared our ministry philosophy and was further down the road than we were in building remuneration into their program. In January 2010, three HWI board members and Ken, our probable trike contract worker, met in

Central Florida for two days, along with a donor and businessman from Texas.

The meeting was successful on several counts. I-TEC offered to help market our trike by having one on display in their showroom for their constituents to see. Our team was able to hone the trike ministry focus. We also decided to hire Ken in a contracting position for forty hours a month.

Before returning home, I spent a few hours debriefing with God while enjoying some prayer time and silence amid His creation at a state park in Florida. There I reflected on His grandeur and absorbed His wonders as He solidified His leading in my soul. I knew from experience, as well as from the biblical account of Elijah, that after such a ministry high, I would likely face the low of spiritual discouragement when I finally reached home. And indeed I did, in the form of familiar doubts: "How can I lead HWI forward while dealing with such a debilitating condition?" Once again I had to remind myself to continue "drafting off God."

Days after I returned home, God continued affirming our faith moves. This time He used the words of a church leader and businessman. "I'm constantly amazed by your stories," he said. "I don't think you're two-faced, having a love for business every day except Sunday. But every time I see you, God is bringing new business opportunities your way. Somehow you are a person God is doing super spiritual things through." He went on to say that businessmen "know how to make business deals happen, but this isn't about business deals. This is the Holy Spirit's leading."

After we took the leap of faith to bring Ken on as a contract worker, the businessman from Texas who had joined us in Florida sent a check to cover the first few months of Ken's hours. The businessman had heard me speak on the radio in 2006. Afterward he sent in a sizable check with a note enclosed. All the note said was, "God bless your ministry." I sent a personal letter back, thanking him. He continued sending periodic checks over the next couple years.

Another exciting affirmation came through Jeremy, the humanitarian worker who was building trikes in North Africa. After distributing the initial six in 2008, he had said, "All six recipients came dragging themselves through the filthy sand on their hands, but they left in a 'flashy' fast trike, which provided dignity and hope." Two years later, he had completed his goal of manufacturing twenty trikes.

While Jeremy was finishing the remaining fourteen trikes at the beginning of 2010, a representative of the Tunisian Embassy who had been a client at the fitness center he ran there saw him assembling trikes and started asking questions. Jeremy said, "He expressed some interest in the trikes and then came back to me a day or two later. He said he would like to purchase ten of them to be given away at a future charitable event to be held by the Tunisian Embassy. I only had eight left, but I sold them all to him."

At the end of March, during a vision-casting budget meeting, we again discussed our need to "move on down the road." Afterward our accountant said, "There is some property nearby. I'll go and investigate." He returned with the address and telephone number, and sure enough, it was the same place I'd prayed outside of when I saw the "For Rent" sign.

By then I had prayed 374 hours over the past six months. I made the cold call. After the secretary answered, I introduced myself. But her voice sounded familiar.

She interrupted me and asked, "Do you remember me?"

I was shocked to learn that this woman I'd known in my college days was the landlord's administrative assistant. She told me some things about the landlord's stellar reputation.

Within fifteen minutes Kevin, Ken, and I went to meet the landlord and to see the property. I soon learned the landlord was the cousin of one of the five missionaries martyred in Ecuador in the 1950s.

I told him, "I'm a rookie at this and don't know what I am doing here other than following God's lead."

As we continued talking, the landlord encouraged us. Then we hit a potential snag. He wanted a four-year lease, but I said, "I don't know if we are going to go boom or bust. What if we go bust and we've signed a four-year lease?"

He said, "You won't go bust, but if at any time you want to terminate the lease, you can do so without explanation or penalty." My jaw dropped. I had been warned that signing a lease is equivalent to an ongoing debt. After parting ways, the landlord and I did our homework and researched each other.

With my emotions swirling, I shared the plans with my brother, Dan. "I don't know what I'm doing or if these dreams are going to become a reality."

Dan said, "Do you want it to happen? If you want it to happen, it will happen!" My brother was encouraging me to go for my dreams and not let fear or ambivalence keep me from what God wanted to do in and through me.

I also consulted with the businessman from Texas. "I am confident about where HWI is going," he said, "because HWI's leader is spending time before the Lord in prayer and guiding the ministry from there. I'm sure I could shoot holes into the idea of going ahead with the space as a business deal, but this isn't a business deal. This is an act of faith."

Now I understood that if such a dream were to become a reality, it would require much prayer. It was no wonder God had challenged me to pray eighty hours in March and one hundred hours in April. On April 1, 2010, I planned to begin a grant search to secure funds for our move, having taken an extensive grant-writing course a few years earlier. God's plans were different, however. He challenged me to stay home and to pray forty hours beginning on Maundy Thursday through Easter Sunday, relying on the most powerful fund-raising tool available.

In my prayer journal I wrote, "Lord, George Mueller said he wouldn't ask anyone for money but he would pray, knowing God would provide. I stand on the fence of this method, because it seems impossible. Yet it is much more freeing to come before You in prayer than to go looking for funds as an act of futility. I will pray. Lord, make the steps I am to follow clear, and I will follow."

George Mueller was born in Prussia in 1805 and later moved to Bristol, England, where he spent more than sixty years involved in philanthropic work. He was known for relying on God through prayer for the funds needed to live and do God's work. "He accordingly abolished pew-rents, refused to take a fixed salary, or to appeal for contributions towards his support . . . and he resolved never to incur debt either for personal expenses or in religious work, and never to lay up money for the future."[66] Yet God provided. "No matter how pressing was the need, George simply renewed his prayers, and either money or food always came in time to save the situation."[67]

Mueller's work included educating and sending out into the world "no fewer than 123,000 pupils; he circulated 275,000 Bibles in different languages, with nearly as many smaller portions of Scripture; and he aided missions to the extent of 255,000£ [a vast sum in his day]. He supported 189 missionaries, and he employed 112 assistants."[68]

Mueller also began his first orphanage in 1836 and his fifth one in 1872. He, along with the other workers, raised more than ten thousand orphans over the course of fifty-seven years.

As I thought about the challenge to go forward in faith, I was both excited and afraid. When I talked to people about Mueller's style of ministry, the common reply was, "The style of ministry that Mueller practiced just won't work today. These are different days."

Our regular donor contributions were under $100 a month. Yet God continued to challenge me to move forward in faith. It didn't make sense, but what were my options? I faced a crisis as I considered the logical counsel of my consultants in contrast to God's faith plan. Yet God confirmed His plan from many directions. Jen, my friend and accountability partner, said, "Why wouldn't you proceed by faith? It is consistent with how you've lived most of your life, and God has blessed you."

My psychologist said, "I don't hear anything but perfect peace in your voice. If anyone else told me such news, I would have great hesitation and doubt. However, I know this is the way God works in your life. This is your lifestyle, and God has honored and blessed it. He has used your life as a powerful testimony for His glory. Hold on to this peace when you find yourself doubting."

The Lord also continued confirming His plan during Maundy Thursday's prayer time, as I read the following quote from George Mueller:

> *If once we have, in submission to the teaching of the Spirit in the word, taken hold of God's promise, and believed that the Father has heard us, we must not allow ourselves by any delay or unfavorable appearances be shaken in our faith. . . . When once satisfied that anything which they bring before God in prayer, is according to His will, ought to continue in believing, expecting, persevering prayer until the blessing is granted.*[69]

I sensed the Holy Spirit saying, "You are going out to look for money that has already been given to you. Use your own money to move forward. I, the Lord, will provide."

I went on to pray, "Oh, Lord, confirm Your plans, and show us as a board how to proceed." As I continued praying, I asked myself, *If I believe God is calling us forward, am I willing to risk all for obedience?*

On Good Friday, as I continued another ten hours in prayer, a quote from William Blaikie shot like an arrow to my heart.

> *When we have clear indications of the Divine mind as to any course of action, we are to advance to it promptly and without fear, even though the means at our disposal appear utterly inadequate. . . . If God really is our Master, all the resources of heaven and earth are at our back. . . . If we waver in our trust in Him, if we fly to the resources of human policy . . . we arrest, as it were, the electric current flowing from heaven, and become weak as other men.*[70]

The last thing I wanted was to live a life of safety, relying on my own security and thereby forfeiting the blessings of obeying God's call.

Throughout the weekend I sensed God saying, "If you aren't willing to trust Me and take a leap of faith by pursuing the rental property, then His Wheels will not grow any further." I knew that Scripture is clear about remaining debt free, and it also states, "Yours, O LORD, is the greatness and the power and the glory and the victory and the majesty, for all that is in the heavens and in the earth is yours. . . . Both riches and honor come from you, and you rule over all."[71] I realized that my only option was to trust God, moving forward in faith and relying on Him to cover our bills. He could provide all HWI's needs just as He had provided mine. If we were unable to meet our financial responsibilities, then we would have to terminate our lease. But I couldn't confuse obedience with fear or failure.

On Saturday of Holy Week, after ten hours of prayer, I attended an Easter vigil service. There God again affirmed that He wanted my obedience as I heard the story of Abraham's willingness to sacrifice his son Isaac. Abraham was willing to obey, even though it meant surrendering his beloved son—his joy and his heir—as well as the promise from God to become the father of many nations. Yet Abraham was faithful. He said, "I and the boy will go over there and worship and come again to you."[72]

I concluded my forty hours of prayer on Easter Sunday by journaling, "Doing God's work requires turning my insecurity and timidity over to Him. I have often let my fear of whether others would reject me, laugh at me, or accuse me scare me off from obeying God."

I was confident God wanted HWI to move forward. Now I could look back and see how He had chiseled away at my financial fears over the past decade. But two human obstacles still remained before moving forward in faith and signing a lease. One was the need for approval from the zoning board to do the type of ministry we had in mind at the new facility. The other was the approval of the His Wheels board.

I was still yet to learn that Pray 10K was God's road map. It was complete with the necessary how-to instructions for the next move down the road for HWI . . . and for my own journey.

The Last Mile . . . for Now

As I reflected on His Wheels International's journey up to this point, I found myself reliving the last mile of my second cross-country trip. The excitement was building. We had just announced to the nation via *The 700 Club* television show that our team had accomplished our mission—cycling from California to Virginia.

We'd been across the United States, and now the people in Norfolk, Virginia, were welcoming us as we approached the completion of our trip. Our team was filled with contagious energy, which the TV cameras and newspaper photographers were attempting to capture as we approached Virginia Beach. As the spectators encountered sixty riders with eyes fixated on the ocean and energy that rocked the shoreline, they must have wondered, *What is going on?* With tunnel vision and fierce determination, I made my way to the water with my teammates.

Now, during our April 2010 annual board meeting, we voted unanimously to move forward on the new rental space. The energy in my soul was at the same magnitude it had been back in 1978 as I approached the Atlantic Ocean. But first we needed clearance from the zoning board. The meeting would take place four days after our board meeting. Within minutes of the beginning of the zoning meeting, we got the approval. Afterward I notified the board. The following day I signed the lease.

Within hours of signing the lease, Kevin began moving trike inventory into the building. Time was running short. Ten days later we had to ship out our first order of fifteen trike kits to Soddo Christian Hospital in Ethiopia, an order they had placed almost eight weeks earlier. Kevin began the intensive process of visually laying out more than one hundred different parts, rechecking them, then building and packing the crate.

Shipping trikes to Ethiopia was a dream that had begun in 2005, with the Ethiopian government official who had said, "We need trikes throughout Africa." It had been rekindled in 2007, when I met Carolyn and Dr. Adolph, both part of Soddo Christian Hospital. Further brainstorming about starting a vocational rehabilitation workshop on the hospital compound took place over the months I was in Florida during 2008 and 2009. Finally, Dr. Adolph had a connection with a welder in Ethiopia who could fabricate the trikes.

Soddo Christian Hospital was an ideal partner in distributing the trikes. For one thing, they had an orthopedic surgeon who helped determine the recipients. He considered the individuals' needs and ability to pedal a trike and then selected the best candidates from his patient base. The hospital was also a teaching site for the Pan-African Academy of Christian Surgeons (PAACS), a five-year surgical training program that educated and trained African doctors to become surgeons. Having the trikes at the hospital would increase visibility throughout the world, as visiting professors and surgeons from many nations provided surgical courses for the African doctors there.

During the days following the signing of the lease, fireworks of blessing continued going off. On April 21, the day after signing the lease, I got an unexpected call from a local foundation. "We have just approved a $5,000 grant for HWI." No one within HWI had applied for the grant.

The following day our landlord said, "You can design your building sign, and I will buy it and put it up."

The next day, April 23, my forty-eighth birthday, all I could do was give thanks to God for what He had done and celebrate like never before.

But days after getting the crate of trikes off, my spiritual high plummeted, only to be replaced by the surfacing financial fears. Before we signed the lease, we had made a budget and had a good idea what our monthly expenses would average. Expenses would far exceed 2009's income of $40,000. We knew our meager savings would last only about three months and then we would have to rely on faith, not funds. But now I was starting to have doubts. What had I gotten us into by signing a lease? I questioned the sound decision I had made in the light as the dark cloud of fear rolled in.

I had to take my place on HWI's team peloton, praying forty hours over another weekend in May. I ran into

God's arms and hid myself in the shelter of His wings. I prayed, "My heart is paralyzed by the fear of finances and a lack of faith. I've been in this place before and can recount all the ways You saw me through. Bind Satan and keep me from entertaining his subtle messages. Uproot the cause of this financial fear." Afterward I felt the Lord say,

In the past when people asked, "How are you going forward financially?" you didn't have an answer. I led and cared for you then, as I am doing now. The world is looking for worldly answers. I am God over this move, as I have been over each part of HWI's ministry. I don't always answer in ways that satisfy earthly questions. Trust and obey Me alone. It is the only way forward. I will see you through in My magnanimous way. Behold the glory and majesty of the Lord Most High. I am your Redeemer and Lord, Alice.

As I clung to the sovereignty of God, He replaced my frenzied anxiety with His perfect peace.

By the end of May, I was able to make room in my soul for our new headquarters as an amazing gift and adventure, an investment in the greatest "bike trip" of my life. I knew the "trail fee" would require sacrifice, but I had been given a great ministry privilege through HWI. This verse from Isaiah sealed my new adventure: "Thus says the LORD, your Redeemer, the Holy One of Israel: 'I am the LORD your God, who teaches you to profit, who leads you by the way you should go.'"[73]

In June, just seven weeks after moving in, we had an open house, where ninety-one people dropped by. They celebrated with us and participated in a time of praying, sharing, and dedicating our headquarters to God. Sparked by the open house, four teenagers began volunteering during our summer mechanic days. One mother wrote to me:

When I told my fifteen-year-old daughter I wanted her to volunteer, she was less than enthusiastic. However, after two days of volunteering at HWI, she spent the next afternoon dismantling an old bike in our basement. I will never forget the look of confidence on her face as she showed me how to remove a bike tire. She also asked for bicycle tools for her upcoming birthday. I am thrilled that my daughter is developing new interests and skills, and even more thrilled that she has an opportunity to see God work and take part in a ministry.

It caused me to think back on my own teen years. *Oh, how I wish a ministry like HWI had been around when I was a teen. Then I could have volunteered and learned to repair bikes. It would have saved my dad and me from our numerous silent car rides to Jake's Bike Shop.* On a deeper note, I could have seen much sooner that God was molding my passion and wanted to use it for His glory, not just for my gratification.

The next big event took place three weeks later when HWI participated in Wheaton's Fourth of July parade. We had nineteen people from seven churches volunteer to distribute more than three thousand pieces of HWI literature.

During the fall of 2010, I spoke on three national radio programs. One listener wrote,

My husband was an athletic thirty-three-year-old man when he was diagnosed with a slow-growing bone cancer. He went from being an active, life-long participant in various sports to a disabled man who would never walk again without the aid of crutches or a wheelchair. It has been difficult for him. As I listened to you on the radio, my heart absolutely resonated. I believe my husband will be so encouraged to hear your testimony and challenged to not give up his dreams of being used to minister for the Lord.

Here was another affirmation that God was using bicycle transportation to facilitate life transformation, which He had done for me as well. Gradually the Lord was redeeming my "thorn in the flesh."

On December 31, as we said good night to 2010 in Illinois, HWI was simultaneously welcoming in January 1, 2011, at Soddo Christian Hospital in Ethiopia. The container with our trike crate had arrived, completing our last Ethiopian mile for now.

It also marked the beginning of yet another new adventure as the first trike went to a man named Melesse to replace his old, locally made trike. The orthopedic surgeon had bought Melesse the old trike years earlier, and it had confirmed to the surgeon the value of such a trike for those with similar disabilities.

As payment for the first trike, Melesse volunteered in the hospital. With the ability to speak eight languages, Melesse became the surgeon's translator, facilitating communication between the surgeon, patients, and family members. This second time around Melesse would pay for his new HWI trike the same way he had paid for his first—continuing to work at the hospital. I couldn't think of a more exciting way to end 2010 and begin 2011.

Back in 1988, when I'd said, "God, I will go with You wherever You lead," I never guessed He would take me on an uncharted, life-transforming journey of the heart. Back then I wasn't afraid of going to another country. But I would have feared embarking on a journey of giving Him total control of my heart and all my other resources.

As I looked back on 2010, I was amazed to see all God had done. HWI had provided 1,400 bikes and trikes to individuals affiliated with eighty-five countries. My total clocked prayer time since 1988 were more than seven thousand hours. Looking back, I was glad I'd chosen to dangerously live out my God-given dreams, embracing and grappling with the tensions involved, and refusing a life of mediocrity, safety, discontentment, and fear.

As I look ahead, I'm unsure what the future holds. But I know God has a future for His Wheels International— and for me. As an organization we are refining our vision to focus more of our energy into the trike field. After designing twenty-one different trike prototypes, consulting with other organizations that work with the disabled, and interacting with manufacturers, we are discovering there is considerable energy being directed to trikes all around the world.

Many individuals have a passion to help the disabled and have turned their garages into trike workshops. As HWI has grown in visibility and as we have spent more than five years doing research and development, many people have contacted us to find out more about our design. We are seeing that those who have the ability to design have not always considered the ergonomic concerns to prevent overuse problems for the end user.

HWI is on the cusp of finding overseas partners and moving forward with our dream of sending kits for fabricating trikes, as well as the manufacturing fixtures needed to begin small factory production sites in other countries.

Through the first part of my journey as HWI's founder and executive director, I've uncovered another interest of mine—mentoring leaders. This passion has taken shape while speaking and working alongside groups like the Boy Scouts, Pioneer Girls, and graduate students. I've had the privilege of navigating life with them as we've worked together. Students have asked about my faith as they have seen God answer many prayers. Others have asked how I handle the unknown future of my health, while at the same time directing a ministry forward.

While working, we have gotten our hands dirty together. It is often there that scary life issues have a place to surface. It doesn't take long before they hear or see how Christ continues refining my life through the crucible of suffering with CFS. Through word and example, I have the privilege of being an agent of transformation, as both a student and leader. I long to continue helping others find their dreams and then stand by as they launch into making those dreams a reality.

The ultimate longing of my heart is that "the tested genuineness of your faith—more precious than gold that perishes though it is tested by fire—may be found to result in praise and glory and honor at the revelation of Jesus Christ."[74] Through my journey, where at times there have been no human solutions, I have witnessed the almighty God performing countless miracles on my behalf. I echo the words of Charles H. Spurgeon:

If you cannot travel, remember that our Lord Jesus Christ is more glorious than all else that you could ever see. Get a view of Christ and you have seen more than mountains and cascades and valleys and seas can ever show you. Earth may give its beauty, and stars their brightness, but all these put together can never rival Him.[75]

Indeed, through the great adventure of following Christ while being challenged by a disability, I have seen more than I ever would have seen if I had fulfilled my own dream of cycling through all fifty states and on all seven continents. This adventure has left me feeling much like I did during the climax of my trip in 1978, dipping my front wheel into the Atlantic Ocean. I had mixed emotions as I heard, "Congratulations! You did it," knowing this was "the end . . . for now." I'm not sure where the road will lead, but I pray I'll always be up for another trip.

God, the Ultimate Dream Weaver

For years I tried to wipe out the promise my twin brother, Dan, had made in high school: "When I get rich, I will buy you a bicycle shop." Since dreaming had never come easily for me, it took years to recognize that his words were my dream. In acknowledging this, I faced a soul resistance that alerted me to the power of dreaming.

I felt the weight of reaching my dream and feared the transformation that would have to occur before I could take hold of my dream. But whenever my brother reminded me of his promise, a flutter of excitement touched my heart. In difficult times throughout my adolescence and early adulthood, I found myself returning to that exhilarating place in my heart, full of raw imagination.

There I encountered doubt and worry, and succumbed to the fear of failure and being misunderstood. My refusal to admit to and articulate such a foolish-sounding idea blocked my imagination from soaring and thereby giving wings to my dream. Before I could even start imagining such a reality, I had to undergo major heart and soul reconstruction.

After God began reconstructing my heart and soul, I had the guts to believe that I was made to dream and deserved to embrace dreams as gifts from God. I created time before the Lord, where I turned off the outside noise and demands from others, allowing God to uncover my unique personality, passions, and gifts. I stopped rushing around and doing everything that sounded good, so I could refocus my energy to embrace what was good deep inside—my dreams.

I needed tenacious determination to face the barriers that had so often squelched the tender shoot of my imagination from taking root in the past. But over the years, those dreams never really left. They reappeared in an unlikely place—in the midst of my daily struggles with CFS.

God's perfect timing for my dreams to bud and grow was during what looked to the rest of the world like the ultimate worst time—when my financial means were slim and the United States was facing one of the deepest recessions since the Great Depression. His Wheels had less than $15,000 in the bank and only a few regular givers, amounting to $100 in expected monthly income.

It was during that time that I sensed the Lord say, "Be willing to pay the price for your dream by signing the lease and moving HWI out of your home. If you don't step out in faith, His Wheels will not grow any further."

There I faced a fork in the road. One way led down the road of complacency, which would allow fear to win again. The other way required turning onto the road of dangerous abandonment. Making the turn toward my dreams required action—uncovering my passions, embracing them, and then living them out. It also took perseverance to reach my potential in Christ. Prayer was the fuel that powered this vehicle for self-discovery, personal growth, spiritual maturity, and leadership development. As I pen these words at the beginning of April 2012, I have now prayed 9,300 of the 10,000 hours that began in 1988, with the goal to pray one hour a week.

The day I turned the key in our HWI headquarters, I felt a surge of adrenaline course through my body, along with the sensation that I was receiving the gift of a lifetime. It was beyond my wildest imagination of a bicycle shop. When I entered the building, I felt like I was stepping into a place where adventure, joy, and discovery awaited me.

The cost of uncovering my dreams, which had been paid through my struggles, suffering, and pain, was now all worthwhile. At last my heart was set free to marvel in the person God had made me to be.

I will never forget the day I showed my family our new headquarters, as my joy bubbled over. When I opened the door, I said, "Dan, how did you do in buying me a bicycle shop?"

We laughed our knowing twin laugh. He said, "I could never have imagined something this big."

Memories flooded my soul. Eleven years earlier, while praying, a friend had said, "I saw a picture of your life as a star. Each of the points was sending out millions of rays of light, shining around the world." Back then it was hard to imagine how God would answer her prayer. Thirteen years earlier, I wondered how God would ever answer my prayer for an enjoyable position whereby I would have variety in my work, utilizing my interests, my talents, my education, and my love for Christ in a God-sized position.

He has done that—and more—as he has fulfilled my prayer from 1998 to expand my imagination for how I could serve Him. He enveloped my brother's promise, the prayers of others, and my own desires and prayers into a God-sized opportunity that still leaves me daily astounded by His miracles.

"This is bigger than what I could ever have dreamed of getting for you, Alice," Dan said. "But it's certainly not too big for you!"

As we left, my nephew, eleven years old at the time, said, "Aunt Alice, your story is like Job's. God took everything from you, and then He gave you more than you could have dreamed about."

As we settled into HWI's headquarters, my "bicycle shop," I began to see that it would be where God would unveil the most intimate and vulnerable places of my heart. In the process I learned that each of the desires, passions, interests, talents, and gifts God had given me throughout my life now had a place for realization, cultivation, and expression.

Only as I continued traversing the unknown road to fulfilling my God-sized dreams could the true beauty of my soul blossom. It would require the continual guidance of the Holy Spirit, the road map of Scripture, and the power of the triune God. My bicycle shop was just the beginning of the God-sized adventure and journey God had in store for me.

As I thought back to that cold, rainy day while cycling through Israel in January 1988, I remember thinking, *I have accomplished all my childhood dreams.* When that thought came over me out of nowhere, my initial feeling was one of elation, knowing I was finally fulfilling my eleven-year dream to bike in Israel. After basking in the accomplishment for a few miles I realized that at the age of twenty-six, I didn't have any dreams left.

It was then that I discovered the power dreams had to propel me forward. I was afraid to consider living the rest of my life without more dreams. I was forced to pause, pray, and ask myself, "Now what? How do I come up with new dreams?"

Before the Israel trip ended, I had come up with the dream to bicycle on all seven continents and through all fifty states. I didn't know how I would accomplish my dream. I remember how foolish I felt when I shared my wild idea. The routine wisecrack response became, "How are you going to bike Antarctica?"

That response intimidated me at first, because it gave way for others to make fun of my dream. The question also presented an insurmountable obstacle I hadn't considered. It required some thought, which only made me embrace my dream all the more with its newfound complexity. It broadened my horizon to dream of somehow combining flying and pedaling. Later, whenever I told people I wanted to bike on all seven continents, I would end by saying, "I am going to worry about the last continent when I get there!"

I may never fulfill my dream of biking on all seven continents and in all fifty states, but through His Wheels I have gone to more places around the world than I ever could have imagined before CFS struck. I am thankful for the privilege of assisting more than 1,500 people, affiliated with six continents and eighty-eight countries, in receiving the gift of transportation through His Wheels. This accomplishment far exceeds the thrill of having fulfilled my human-sized goal of cycling through all those countries.

Dreams are filled with thrills and ills. Shortly after we'd signed our lease, as I finished writing out all the utility bills for our new headquarters, I found myself at a dead end. The bills amounted to $3,600, and we had only $2,000 in our accounts. With just three days left in the month, we still needed $1,600. It was then that Louise, my ninety-two-year-old mentor, reminded me "A faith-based ministry begins when the economic resources end."

At that dead end, with only seventy-two hours left before becoming a "faith-based ministry," God was testing my faith in a whole new way. When I signed the lease, I had sensed the Lord challenging me to proceed by faith, not by asking others for money to support HWI. Now I was being tested in my areas of greatest weakness—my passion for bicycles and my need for finances. All God wanted was my worship, love, and full loyalty.

There I also had to answer the question, "Where do you see HWI headed in the future?" Having to dream bigger than ever before, while being unsure if we would have the money to keep the headquarters open, created a tension-filled dichotomy. I was torn, wondering, *How will HWI continue?* Yet God, the ultimate Dream Weaver, had allowed me to face that tense place—to test my faith and show me that He was trustworthy and true.

I knew God was faithful, even when I reached my wit's end and couldn't imagine His solution to my problems. At that place of both belief and disbelief, I articulated my dreams in a robotic way, unable to imagine how or if they would ever come true. I know that when my faith is tested, God's number-one concern is the transformation of my heart and soul. Each new challenge is an opportunity for a stronger thread of trust to be woven into my life and the lives of those involved in the ministry of HWI.

I never could have imagined how living out my dream would impact others. In his nationally syndicated radio broadcast on January 2, 2012, Chris Fabry made the following comments to set up what he called "a best-of programs from October 2010":

> *You are a difference maker, your heart, your soul, your life. You are making a difference to those around you even if you don't sense it or understand it. . . . This program is going to make a difference in someone's life as we start off the New Year. . . . It deals with a woman who loved something, who had that thing she loved taken away from her and then instead of giving up, she allowed God to give her a new vision of that thing.*
>
> *One reason we wanted to air this in the first broadcast day of the New Year is because in the coming days and weeks, I want to look at people's lives who've been given a dream and who have allowed God to mold that dream in and through them. Because I'm convinced we can either hold on to the vision, the dream we have generated inside of us—what we think that ought to be, what we think life ought to be—or we can allow*

*God to shape that in us to do what He wants. That's what the
story of Alice Teisan is going to teach us today. That's what I
hope you hear coming through loud and clear.*

On the canvas of my life, through the medium of
bicycles and CFS, God has created a beautiful tapestry. He
took my dreams and used them as the highlighting threads, in
which He wove together the desires of my heart. Indeed, He
works all things together for His good.[76] My desire is for my
life, His masterpiece, to glorify His name. I declare as the
psalmist of old did in Psalm 46:

> *Come, behold the works of the LORD. . . .*
> *"Be still, and know that I am God.*
> *I will be exalted among the nations,*
> *I will be exalted in the earth!"*
> *The LORD of hosts is with us;*
> *the God of Jacob is our fortress.*[77]

May we soar on the wings of our dreams as the
ultimate Dream Weaver leads the way!

Introduction

1. What dream or talent has someone else identified for you?

2. How did you respond to the messenger? What made you respond the way you did?

Chapter 1

1. What do you treasure?

2. Describe an incident where you lost something you treasured or where it was stolen from you.

3. Describe how illness or another extenuating circumstance interrupted an important event in your life. How did you process the situation?

Chapter 2

1. Tell about one of your greatest fears and if it has come true.

2. Share a spiritual lesson you have learned and the way you have incorporated it into your everyday life.

3. What are the roadblocks that keep you from admitting, accepting, or pursing your passion?

4. What was your initial dream?

5. What circumstances in life make your dream impossible to fulfill? How could God repurpose your dream in a way that is beyond your expectations?

Chapter 3

1. What is/was your dream of security, and how has it crumbled?

2. Tell us about one of your confidants. How did you meet him or her? How have you kept the friendship going in this hectic world?

3. Share a story of how your confidant has helped or challenged you.

Chapter 4

1. What obstacles or detours have you or are you experiencing?

2. What are your coping mechanisms?

3. Have your lifelong coping mechanisms ever been yanked from you? If so, how did that happen?

4. How have the detours or losses impacted your spiritual/emotional journey?

Chapter 5

1. Have you ever asked, "Why me? Does my life still have a purpose?" If so, what did you wrestle with? What conclusion did you come to?

2. How have you relied on a life verse or other meaningful verses over the years?

3. What price would you have to pay to begin living out your dream?

4. What obstacles are distracting you from your dream?

Chapter 6

1. Share a time when you felt God wanted you to do something and the excuses and obstacles that first had to be dealt with.

2. Hebrew 13:2 says, "Do not neglect to show hospitality to strangers, for thereby some have entertained angels unawares" (ESV). Share a time when you were on the giving or receiving end of such hospitality.

3. Share a difficult experience in your life that in retrospect you wouldn't trade in for an easy road. What treasures or lessons did you gather as a result of that difficult time?

4. Tell of a dream you tried to obliterate and what the outcome was.

Chapter 7

1. Describe a time you felt like God was scrapping a dream of yours and what that dream was?

2. If you have a personal mission statement, share it. If not, what key points would you include in such a statement?

3. Alice shares how her passion for cycling and fixing bikes created a teenage father/daughter challenge. Share a funny or memorable story that gives us insight into your passion.

Chapter 8

1. How has God molded your dreams? What circumstances, people, interests, or events has He used in the process?

2. Has God ever repurposed one of your dreams and woven together threads of your old dream into a new reality? If so, share how.

3. When you think about your passion or dream, what is the Kingdom difference you hope to fulfill by living out your dream?

Chapter 9

1. How has your obedience or disobedience toward God in a particular situation impacted others?

2. Do you still like to dream? If so, share some of your dreams. If not, share what hinders you from dreaming.

3. Whose dream are you living?

2. Do you know people who have lived out their dream? What components of their story do you long for in your life?

Chapter 10

1. When someone compliments you for a job well done, how do you handle the success?

2. What lessons have you learned about handling success, and who did you learn them from?

3. Share with us about one of your friends who holds you accountable.

4. What are your thoughts about this quote by John Maxwell: "The more people you develop, the greater the extent of dreams"?

Chapter 11

1. How has a person with a disability changed your life?

2. In this chapter, after Kevin fits Anika with the racing trike, he says, "I have found what I was created to do!" Share a time when you have felt this way.

3. How are you making a difference to those around you now?

Chapter 12

1. Alice prayed, "I want my life as a leader to be an empty canvas on which God can create a masterpiece that displays His signature." How is God painting the canvas of your life?

2. The stops on Alice's ride were life opportunities. What are the opportunities hidden behind the stops you've taken or are in the midst of now?

3. In what ways are you defined by your job, your titles, or your volunteer roles?

4. After reading this chapter, has your definition of success been changed or challenged?

Chapter 13

1. What have you prayed for, and how is God answering your prayer?

2. Share a joy, struggle, or challenge about your prayer journey.

3. What impossible thing has God challenged you to do in your spiritual life? How did you respond and what were the results?

Chapter 14

1. What fears keep you from turning your dream over to God to shape and use for His Kingdom purposes?

2. "Thus says the LORD, your Redeemer, the Holy One of Israel, 'I am the LORD your God, who teaches you to profit, who leads you in the way you should go'" (Isaiah 48:17, NASB). Share a way this verse has been a reality in your life or the struggles this verse creates for you.

Epilogue

1. Share one of your dreams. What emotions surface when you describe your dream?
2. What price are you willing to pay to fulfill your dream?
3. How are you making a difference to those around you now?
4. In what way has this book touched your life?

Acknowledgments

If I were to acknowledge everyone who helped make my *Riding on Faith* dream a reality, I would miss the majority of you. The gifts, talents, insights, love, and prayers from people of many tribes, tongues, and nations have had a crucial part in making me who I am today. I thank the many teachers and unsung heroes, like Bessie Lippold, who identified the unique strengths in each of us, mentored us, and had the foresight to encourage us to steward our talents for Kingdom purposes. Above all, I stand amazed as I praise the ultimate Dream Weaver, my Abba Father, for beautifully weaving each of these unique threads together.

I'd cherish receiving a note, a picture, a prayer, or a memory from new and old members of my team as a reminder of just how many have had a part in my ongoing *Riding on Faith* journey.

Alice Teisan
His Wheels International
PO Box 423
Wheaton, IL 60187
www.hiswheels.org
info@hiswheels.org

*N*otes

1 Woodrow Michael Kroll, *Bible Country: A Journey through the Holy Land* (Denver: Accent Books, 1982), 105–107.

2 Mark 14:32-37, ESV

3 Psalm 121:1-2, ESV

iv See http://www.ssa.gov/oact/cola/central.html

5 Katrina Berne, PhD, *Chronic Fatigue Syndrome, Fibromyalgia and Other Invisible Illnesses* (Alameda, CA: Hunter House Inc., 2002), 24.

6 See http://consults.blogs.nytimes.com/2009/10/15/readers-ask-a-virus-linked-to-chronic-fatigue-syndrome.

7 See https://listserv.nodak.edu/cgi-bin/wa.exe?A2=ind0006C&L=co-cure&P=R1292

8 Hebrews 13:5, ESV

9 Jill Briscoe, *It Had to Be a Monday* (Carol Stream, IL: Tyndale House Publishers, 1995), 7.

10 Woodrow Michael Kroll, *Bible Country: A Journey through the Holy Land* (Denver: Accent Books, 1982), 72.

11 Ibid.

12 D. Baldwin, MD, endocrinologist at Rush Hospital

13 Psalm 50:10, ESV

14 1 Timothy 5:8, ESV

15 See http://www.dol.gov/whd/regs/compliance/posters/fmlaen.pdf

16 Romans 5:1, NLT

17 Philippians 4:19, ESV

18 1 Chronicles 29:11, ESV

19 Proverbs 22:7, ESV

20 Luke 22:31-32, ESV

21 Proverbs 3:5-6, ESV

[22] "School Desegregation, *West's Encyclopedia of American Law*, 2005,
http://www.encyclopedia.com/topic/School_integration.aspx

[23] 1 Corinthians 9:24, ESV

[24] Matthew 5:43-44, ESV

[25] John 8:32, ESV

[26] Philippians 4:10-20, NIV

[27] Luke 1:45, NLT

[28] Zechariah 4:6, KJV

[29] See
http://womenshistory.about.com/od/quotes/a/qu_anais_nin.htm

[30] Psalm 37:4, ESV

[31] See http://verylocaldata.com/counties/IL/dupage

[32] Eunice Russell Schatz, *The Slender Thread: Stories of Pioneer Girls' First 25 Years* (Mukilteo, WA: Winepress Publishing, 1996), 26.

[33] Ibid., 31.

[34] "Christian Journalism Pioneer Robert Walker Dies," Evangelical Press Association, 2008,
http://www.epassoc.org/index.php?option=com_content&task=view&id=207&Itemid=168.

[35] See http://www.christianitytoday.com/help/features/faq.html

[36] See
http://www.christianitytoday.com/help/features/ctimission.html

[37] Joshua 1:9, ESV

[38] See http://riseinternational.org

[39] Jeremiah 1:5, ESV

[40] Peter F. Drucker, *Managing the Non-Profit Organization* (New York: HarperCollins, 1990), 161.

[41] Peter F. Drucker, quoted in Steven Kerr, *Ultimate Rewards* (Boston: Harvard Business School Publishing, 1997), 59.

[42] See http://www.city-data.com/city/Lost-Springs-Wyoming.html

[43] 1 Peter 3:15, ESV

[44] Matthew 6:21, ESV

[45] C. H. Spurgeon, *The Treasury of the Old Testament*, vol. 4 (London: Hunt, Barnard & Co., Ltd.), 524.

[46] Psalm 18:19, ESV

[47] Nancy Klimas, The National Forum, "CFS/FMS Scientific Overview, http://www.ncf-net.org/forum/klimas.htm

[48] John Maxwell, *Developing the Leader within You* (Nashville: Thomas Nelson, 1993).

[49] Joshua 1:9, ESV

[50] Genesis 39:23, NLT

[51] Genesis 1:31, ESV

[52] David H. Stern, *Jewish New Testament Commentary* (Clarksville, MD: Jewish New Testament Publications, 1996), 39.

[53] See http://www.joniand friends.org/static/uploads/PDFs/bio_joni.pdf

[54] 1 Kings 17:2-8, ESV

[55] Genesis 1:31, ESV

[56] Donald Grey Barnhouse, *Genesis: A Devotional Exposition* (Grand Rapids: Zondervan, 1973), 178.

[57] Scott Bowles, "Riding Detroit's 8 Mile," *USA Today*, November 17, 2002, http://www.usatoday.com/life/movies/news/2002-11-07-8mile-cover_x.htm

[58] Psalm 46:10, ESV

[59] 1 Corinthians 3:16-17, ESV

[60] Herbert Lockyer, *All the Prayers of the Bible* (Grand Rapids MI: Zondervan, 1959), 31.

[61] Ephesians 6:12, ESV

[62] 1 Timothy 4:8, ESV

[63] 2 Chronicles 26:5, ESV

[64] Matthew 21:22, KJV

[65] Martin Luther, quote #6, http://www.christian-prayer-quotes.christian-attorney.net

[66] See http://www.wholesomewords.org/biography/bmuller.htm, Christian Biography Resources

[67] Ed Reese, *The Life and Ministry of George Mueller* (Knoxville, TN: Seriesk Reese Publications), http://www.truthfulwords.org/biography/muller.txt

[68] See http://www.wholesomewords.org/biography/bmuller.html

[69] See
http://www.prayerfoundation.org/andres_murray_on_george_m
uller_2.htm
[70] D. D. Blaikie and William Garden, LLD, William Garden, *The Book of Joshua* (Minneapolis: Klock & Klock, 1978), 141–143.
[71] 1 Chronicles 29:11-12, ESV
[72] Genesis 22:5, ESV
[73] Isaiah 48:17, KJV
[74] 1 Peter 1:7, ESV
[75] Richard Ellsworth Day, *The Shadow of the Broad Brim: The Life Story of Charles Haddon Spurgeon, Heir of the Puritans* (Philadelphia: Judson Press, 1934), 226.
[76] Romans 8:28, paraphrased
[77] Psalm 46:8-11, ESV

18181704R00122

Made in the USA
Middletown, DE
25 February 2015